The Spirit of Enthusiasm

A History of the Catholic Charismatic Renewal, 1967–2000

Susan A. Maurer

UNIVERSITY PRESS OF AMERICA,® INC.
Lanham • Boulder • New York • Toronto • Plymouth, UK

Copyright © 2010 by
University Press of America,® Inc.
4501 Forbes Boulevard
Suite 200
Lanham, Maryland 20706
UPA Acquisitions Department (301) 459-3366

Estover Road
Plymouth PL6 7PY
United Kingdom

All rights reserved
Printed in the United States of America
British Library Cataloging in Publication Information Available

Library of Congress Control Number: 2010927617
ISBN: 978-0-7618-5193-6 (paperback : alk. paper)
eISBN: 978-0-7618-5194-3

∞™ The paper used in this publication meets the minimum
requirements of American National Standard for Information
Sciences—Permanence of Paper for Printed Library Materials,
ANSI Z39.48-1992

For my parents, Bill and Helen Maurer

Contents

1 Introduction — 1
2 The History of Pentecostalism in the 20th Century — 8
3 The Duquesne Weekend and the Cursillo Movement — 23
4 The Catholic Charismatic Renewal and Its Relationship with the Church, the Papacy, and Vatican II — 36
5 Changes in the Charismatic Movement in the Late 20th Century — 55
6 Charismatic Spirituality — 63
7 Conclusion — 73

Selected Bibliography — 77

Index — 85

Chapter One

Introduction

The 1960s were a decade of remarkable upheaval in the United States. The civil rights movement demanded equality and justice for blacks in the face of institutionalized segregation and prejudice. The women's liberation movement, spearheaded by authors such as Gloria Steinem, Germaine Greer, and Betty Frieden, encouraged women to demand freedom from traditional roles and social limitations. The involvement of the United States in the cold-war conflict in Vietnam and the corresponding military draft ignited a nationwide movement of resistance and protest among young Americans.

These events all played their parts in setting in motion the dramatic changes that would occur in the United States during the latter half of the 20th Century as young Americans sought to create a society based on ideas of peace, harmony, and freedom. The pivotal year 1967 saw large demonstrations against the Vietnam War in San Francisco and New York City, race riots in Detroit, Newark, Washington D.C., and other U.S. cities, as well as a series of bra-burning demonstrations. Pop culture glorified the use of marijuana and LSD in the belief that these drugs could help users to free their minds and experience higher states of consciousness.

While many of these movements and groups were political in nature, there were others that sought change and renewal in a spiritual sense. In February 1967, a group of Catholic faculty members and students in a spiritual retreat at Duquesne University in Pittsburgh experienced what they called a "baptism in the Spirit." The experience of the "Duquesne Weekend" spread rapidly to other college campuses in the Midwest and then throughout the United States. Soon, the nascent movement came under the leadership of Steve Clark and Ralph Martin, both of whom had been deeply influenced by the Cursillo movement, which had originated in Spain during the 1940's with the purpose of renewing the Roman Catholic Church through the spiritual renewal of individuals. Clark and Martin were influential members of the Ann Arbor Cursillo community; under their leadership, the Catholic Charismatic Renewal (hereafter referred to as CCR) became a strong movement within the Catholic Church. It enjoyed the support of Cardinal Leon Joseph Suenens, Archbishop of Malines-Brussels and Primate of Belgium, who visited with the CCR at Notre Dame University in 1973. Between the years 1974 and 1986, Cardinal Suenens also composed a series of six documents that helped to articulate guidelines and policies for the movement. The movement also had the support of Popes Paul VI and John Paul II, and it continues to enjoy the support of Pope Benedict XVI.

This book examines the historical development of the American Catholic Charismatic Renewal from the early influences of the Spanish Cursillo movement to the initial "baptism in the Spirit" event at Duquesne University in 1967 and its development through the end of the 20th Century. The influence of the Second Vatican Council on the movement is explored as well as changes both within the movement itself and in its relationship with the church. The work also considers similarities to, and differences from, the Protestant Pentecostal movement of the 20th Century.

In the introductory chapter these developments are summarized in historical context, providing an outline of the chapters to follow. In Chapter Two the author presents the historical background of the movement from its beginnings in the Holiness/Pentecostal tradition of the late 19th and 20th centuries and in the earlier Revival movement, which had its origins in John Wesley's (1703-1791) Methodism and his ideas of Christian perfection and sanctification in the Holy Spirit. The immense popularity of the idea of spiritual rebirth found expression in the Pentecostal movement, which had its "official" beginning at the Azusa Street Revival in Los Angeles in 1906, and which continued to gain in popularity such that it became one of the largest and fastest-growing worldwide religious movements of the late 20th Century. Also examined in the second chapter is the global expansion of Pentecostalism, the role of women within the movement, and the sense of empowerment experienced in Pentecostal communities among people traditionally marginalized in the mainline Christian churches.

Chapter Three examines the Cursillo Movement and the Duquesne Weekend in depth, focusing on the case of Patti Gallagher Mansfield. The Roman Catholic Cursillo movement originated on the Spanish island of Mallorca in 1944. The *cursillo,* or "short course," was originally a week-long retreat designed to prepare young men for pilgrimage to the Spanish basilica of Santiago de Campostela. In order for the men to achieve the state of grace deemed appropriate for the pilgrimage, the retreat, with the blessing of Pope Pius XI, included periods of silence, meditation, presentations on spiritual topics, music and singing, and sharing. The cursillos became popular, and eventually a three-day version of the retreat was created which by the 1950's made its appearance in the United States, where it quickly took root and spread throughout the country. Among those who became active in the Cursillo movement were Yale graduate Steve Clark and Notre Dame graduate Ralph Martin. These men would become two of the most influential early organizers of the CCR in the United States.

The third chapter contains a review of the events at the January 1967 Chapel Hill interdenominational prayer meeting that took place at the home of a "Spirit-filled Presbyterian,"[1] Flo Dodge. The author describes the effects that this meeting had on two of the four Catholics who attended and later organized the weekend student retreat at Duquesne which would mark the birth of the CCR in the United States. The author also examines the case of Patti Gallagher Mansfield, who was a participant in the 1967 Duquesne Weekend retreat and who later became, and remains, a committed spokesperson for the CCR.

A very significant event of the 1960s was the Second Vatican Council (1962-1965), convened by Pope John XXIII for the purpose of renewal of the church so that it could "look to the future without fear."[2] Therefore, in Chapter Four this investigator examines the Second Vatican Council and the relationship of this council to the emerging Charismatic movement. It explores the dynamic between the CCR and the church hierarchy and the principles of the Second Vatican Council (1962-1965). Specifically reviewed are the responses of the papacy, as well as the Catholic clergy and laity, to the movement during the period of the council and through the end of the twentieth century.

The chapter opens by considering the mood of the church and the laity during the period preceding the council. It proceeds through the effects of Pope John XXIII's call for *Aggiornamento*, or the work of bringing the church into the modern world in a way that would renew the church's pastoral relationship with the faithful and imbue the church with the spirit of "a new Pentecost." This expression of Pope John XXIII was understood by some members of the Catholic laity as a validation of their experiences of having been "baptized in the Spirit." In this chapter, the researcher especially emphasizes the efforts of Cardinal Leon Joseph Suenens of Belgium to keep the movement within the embrace of the church as he acted as a liaison between the movement's founders and the Vatican. Cardinal Suenens' participation validated the Renewal and added credibility to its identity as a movement located firmly within the church. Resistance to the movement within the church is also examined here. Additionally, in Chapter Four the author studies the responses of three Popes (Paul VI, John Paul II, and Benedict XVI) to the CCR. The chapter concludes with an analysis of the present status of the movement and its current relationship with the Roman Catholic Church.

Chapter Five traces the subsequent history of the CCR, focusing especially on changes that occurred within the movement during the latter years of the 20th Century, when the movement appeared to some to begin to decline. The author considers whether the movement actually did begin to weaken as has been claimed, or whether it simply underwent a subtle but important transformation.

As a movement based on a personal relationship with the Holy Spirit, the CCR is characterized by, and places high priority on, perceived manifestations, or gifts (charisms) of the Spirit such as *glossolalia* (speaking in tongues), prophecy, and physical and/or spiritual healing. Accordingly, in the Sixth Chapter the author examines the nature of Charismatic spirituality, comparing and contrasting it with earlier Catholic forms of mysticism as well as with the spirituality of the American Pentecostal movement. The investigator seeks to understand the meaning and the effects of "renewal in the Spirit" for those who have experienced it and who continue to live that experience.

In Chapter Seven the author presents conclusions about the CCR. In this chapter the history of the movement is summarized and an understanding of the origins, development, and changes within the movement is offered. Also suggested are possible reasons for the emergence of the movement at the particular historical and social juncture in which it was born, and questions are raised about the future of the movement and the possible directions the movement appears to be taking as it progresses through the 21st century.

THE SOCIAL AND RELIGIOUS ENVIRONMENT OF THE 1960s

As has been stated, the 1960s were a period of remarkable social and political upheaval, not only in the United States, but throughout the world. The end of World War II, arguably the deadliest and most destructive war in human history, left the United States, with losses of 330,000 troops and virtually no civilian deaths, in the most advantageous and politically dominant position of its short history. In contrast, China experienced 3.1 million military casualties and 9 million civilian deaths, Poland experienced 2.5 million civilian deaths, Greece lost 400,000 civilians, and Yugoslavia lost 1.3 million civilians, in addition to 320,000 military casualties. Germany lost 3.5 million troops and 2 million civilians.[3] America's post-war economy was booming and Americans were optimistic and confident, seeing "their victory in war as proof of the superiority of their way of life."[4]

The Soviet Union, on the other hand, had suffered more casualties than any other nation during the Second World War—7.5 million military deaths and between 15 and 20 million civilian deaths.[5] Josef Stalin, who had rejected the Marshall Plan for the Soviet Union as well as its satellite countries in Eastern Europe, distrusted the West in general and in particular the United States, which had recently dropped two nuclear bombs on Japan. The United States and the Soviet Union became engaged in a nuclear arms race which meant that any move toward war on the part of either would result in tremendous, possibly nuclear, destruction. Unwilling to engage in a nuclear battle, the two countries engaged in a political standoff known as the "Cold War," which involved the proliferation of nuclear arsenals, political intrigue, and competition for control of smaller, weaker nations. The Truman Doctrine, which promised American support to any nation that opposed communism, deepened the polarization between the two countries and resulted in a series of proxy wars fought in the nations of the "Third World." Korea, Cuba, the Middle East, and Vietnam all suffered the consequences of the struggle between communism and democracy.

The Cold War, that terrifying confrontation between the capitalist and democratic (and predominantly Christian) United States and the atheistic communist Soviet Union, reached its most critical moment in the Cuban Missile Crisis of 1962, where the refusal of the Soviet Union to abandon construction of nuclear missile sites in Cuba and the refusal of the United States to back down in its threat to invade Cuba if the Soviets did not comply brought the two powers to the brink of nuclear war.

Among the proxy wars fought between the forces of democracy and communism, the Vietnam confrontation brought about the greatest public reaction in the United States. Opposed to the involvement of the United States in the conflict, and to the Selective Service System (military draft) which inducted over 1,700,000 between 1964 and 1973,[6] protesters gathered in large and frequent anti-war demonstrations throughout the United States.

In addition to the tense international political situation, the civil rights movement in the United States, which sought freedom and equal civil rights for all Americans regardless of race, and the feminist movement, which demanded the liberation of women from their traditional domestic roles, dominated the national consciousness. The "Sixties Generation" was a generation of people born into the prosperity of a post-WWII America that appeared to have failed in its efforts to bring about a peaceful world. It was a generation of seekers searching for meaning in a world where meaning seemed lacking. The mood was either idealistic or cynical, and society was sharply divided by age: the "hippie" generation versus the "establishment." Why? Jack Whalen writes that,

> The sixties youth revolt was in part about the possibility of redefining "adulthood" in our society. If a single theme united the otherwise disparate forms of

political and cultural protest that characterized the period, it was the romantic belief that the young could make themselves into new persons, that they need not follow in their parents' footsteps, that they could build lives in which they could exercise a degree of self-mastery not given by the established structures of role, relationship, and routine . . . From another angle, the great personal hope of the sixties was that one would be able to live a life of ongoing self-examination, a life of scrutinizing the moral content of one's actions, a life grounded in principle and social responsibility, a life of service, care, and commitment to justice and social betterment.[7]

Many in the Sixties generation rejected "establishment" values, and they began a quest for "a life grounded in principle." The resulting spiritual dynamic played an important role in launching the civil rights movement, the feminist movement, and the anti-war movement.

But there was something else. The search for a life that could be redefined as grounded in values different from, and perhaps better than, those of preceding generations led a number of people to the conclusion that the meaning of life could not be discerned from the material world. Instead, a "spiritual search" seemed to hold a much greater promise for a generation that was disillusioned by the perceived failure of established institutions and structures to provide a sense of meaning and purpose in a world living under the threat of nuclear annihilation. Western seekers looked to spiritual paths from earlier times and other places, and the ancient Hindu and Buddhist spiritual traditions of India, for example, were imported and adapted to Western needs and expectations. Martin Luther King was inspired by the *satyāgraha*[8] philosophy of Mahatma Gandhi, and he adapted Gandhi's method of *ahimsa*, or non-violent resistance, successfully in his own efforts to improve the condition of African-Americans in the United States. The Beatles' relationship with the Maharishi Mahesh Yogi and their adoption of Indian styles in clothing and music helped to popularize Indian ideas among Western youths. College campuses during the 1960s were alive with protests, "sit-ins," visiting gurus, and spiritual events of many kinds. Eknath Easwaran, a Fulbright Scholar from Kerala, India, conducted the first "for credit" college course in meditation at the University of California in 1960.

But while college campuses were centers of hippie activity and spiritual and psychological experimentation, not everyone turned to Eastern spirituality. There were some who, committed to their Catholic faith and the Roman Catholic Church, sought answers in the ancient wisdom of their own tradition. Organizations such as the *Chi Rho* Society at Duquesne University came into being as "an alternative to sorority and fraternity life." *Chi Rho* was a group of Catholic students who met "to experience Christian fellowship" and the organization had "a strong emphasis on social action." The members met to pray together and to study Scripture. Some of the members of *Chi Rho*, including French major Patti Gallagher Mansfield, attended a weekend spiritual retreat in February of 1967. It was this weekend retreat that would come to be known as the "Duquesne Weekend." It marks the genesis of the CCR in the United States.[9]

Catholics were not the first to engage in the quest for spiritual renewal and a personal relationship with the Holy Spirit. American Protestants had, since the days of the Great Awakenings and the Holiness movement, experienced waves of spiritual enthusiasm that led, early in the 20th century to the emergence of the Pentecostal movement, which would become a global phenomenon and with which the early Catholic Charismatics were familiar. It is with the development of Pentecostalism that this story begins.

NOTES

1. Patti Gallagher Mansfield, a participant in the original Duquesne Weekend of 1967 (accessed 8 June 2006); available from: http://www.ccr.org.uk/duquesne.htm; Internet.

2. Address of Pope John XXIII at the opening of the Second Vatican Council, October 11, 1962 (accessed 10 September 2008); available from: http://www.saint-mike.org/library/Papal_Library/JohnXXIII/Opening_Speech_VaticanII.html; Internet.

3. World War II: Combatants and Casualties (1937 - 45). Web site of Professor Joseph V. O'Brien, Department of History , John Jay College of Criminal Justice (accessed 27 July 2008); available at: http://web.jjay.cuny.edu/~jobrien/reference/ob62.html; Internet.

4. Wayne C. McWilliams and Harry Piotrowski, *The World Since 1945: A History of International Relations* (Boulder: Lynne Rienner Publishers, 2005), 24.

5. Ibid.

6. Web page of the 15th Field Artillery Regiment. Data (accessed 6 June 2008); available from: http://www.landscaper.net/draft70-72.htm#Induction%20Statistics; Internet.

7. Jack Whalen, *Beyond the Barricades: The Sixties Generation Grows Up* (Philadelphia: Temple University Press, 1989), 2.

8. *Satyāgraha*: Sanskrit, literally "force or strength derived from Truth."

9. Patti Gallagher Mansfield, *As By a New Pentecost: The Dramatic Beginning of the Catholic Charismatic Renewal* (Singapore: Noah's Ark Creations Pte Ltd, 1992), 22.

Chapter Two

The History of Pentecostalism in the 20th Century

THE BEGINNINGS

When the day of Pentecost had come, they were all together in one place. And suddenly a sound came from heaven like the rush of a mighty wind, and it filled all the house where they were sitting. And there appeared to them tongues as of fire, distributed and resting on each one of them. And they were all filled with the Holy Spirit and began to speak in other tongues, as the Spirit gave them utterance . . . 'And in the last days it shall be,' God declares, 'that I will pour out my Spirit upon all flesh, and your sons and your daughters shall prophesy, and your young men shall see visions, and your old men shall dream dreams; yea, and on my menservants and my maidservants in those days I will pour out my Spirit; and they shall prophesy.'

Acts 2:1-4,17-18 (RSV)

In 1906 in Los Angeles, an interracial group of Christians under the leadership of a young black pastor came to the notice of the Los Angeles *Times*. Published on April 18, the same day as the occurrence of the great San Francisco earthquake, an article described a vision reported by one of the group's members which prophesied "awful destruction to this city unless its citizens are brought to a belief in the tenets of the new faith." The "new faith" referred to by the Los Angeles *Times* article is what became known as Pentecostalism.[1] This chapter surveys the origins and the development of Pentecostalism, a religious movement that, within a century, grew from a small congregation in Los Angeles to a transnational worldwide phenomenon that is now the fastest-growing Christian movement in the world, and which, according to the *World Christian Database,* comprises at least 25% of the world's Christians.² Some scholars estimate Pentecostal growth at 20 million new members a year; a recent Pew survey estimates the total number of Pentecostals at 500 million worldwide.³ Today, large Pentecostal groups are found not only in the United States and Europe, but also in Brazil, Chile, Guatemala, Kenya, Nigeria, South Africa, India, the Philippines, and South Korea. Some scholars of religious history believe that the movement, which is concentrated and growing fastest in those areas of the world with the most accelerated rates of population growth, may soon become the dominant form of Christianity in the world especially if it continues at its present rate of growth.⁴

The movement commonly known as "Pentecostalism" includes a number (possibly as many as 11,000) of Christian denominations dedicated to several common beliefs. Some of these beliefs are shared with other Evangelical groups and include the importance of direct personal experience of God, acceptance of Jesus as personal savior, and baptism as an outward sign of conversion. However, Pentecostals also place great emphasis on a particular biblical passage, Acts 2:4,⁵ that describes the descent of the Holy Spirit upon the apostles after the ascension of Jesus--an event which bestowed upon them the gift of speaking in foreign tongues (*xenolalia*). Through this gift they would be enabled more effectively to evangelize the world in preparation for the Last Days, when Christ would return to punish sinners, defeat Satan, and establish the Kingdom of Heaven on earth.⁶

Pentecostalism has its roots in the nineteenth-century Holiness revival movement, which originated among Methodists in the United States who, like their founder John Wesley, believed that Christian salvation occurred in two stages. The first, conversion or justification, involved forgiveness from sins committed in the past. The second, sanctification, was the process of total commitment to love of God and avoidance of sin that would result in the full salvation of the believer. Holiness evangelists like Charles Finney, Asa Mahan, and Phoebe Palmer preached to thousands about the need for conversion and sanctification. The camp revivals of the mid-nineteenth century were also a contributing factor to the spread of the dual message of conversion and sanctification.

The movement brought about a split in the Methodist Church between the mainline Methodists and the Holiness Methodists. The Holiness group preached a reactionary revival of the principles of John Wesley. Soon, other Christian denominations became attracted to the message, and independent Holiness sects broke off from mainline Protestant churches.⁷

The idea of sanctification was becoming more popular among Christians, but how was one to know whether the second stage, sanctification, had been achieved? Recalling the events of the second chapter of Acts, Holiness believers began to have dramatic spiritual experiences where they would suddenly feel the Spirit come upon them and bless them with the gift of *xenolalia*. This "baptism of the Holy Spirit," or "second Pentecost,"[8] indicated that the believer had received the gift of sanctification that would also enable them quickly and easily to evangelize foreign populations and bring about their conversion. The idea caught on, and soon more believers claimed to have received the gift. The Pentecostal view of sanctification sharply contrasted with the widespread Evangelical and dispensationalist teaching that the bestowal of the gift had ended along with the age of the apostles.[9]

During the 1890s, Charles Fox Parham, a Methodist from Kansas who believed in the dual conversion/sanctification stages of salvation, began to emphasize a third element in his belief system: the necessity of "baptism with the Holy Ghost and fire." Parham began to preach that speaking in tongues was a necessary part of the sanctification experience. He began to be perceived by some as a modern-day prophet appointed to help prepare the world for the Second Coming.[10] Parham continued to attract interested listeners, and in 1900 he opened a bible school in Topeka, Kansas where he persevered in developing his "Apostolic Faith" theology, which put forward his belief that receivers of the gift of *glossolalia*[11] were charged with evangelizing non-believers in the work of bringing the church age to an end and ushering in the return of Christ.[12]

Parham traveled throughout the United States and even into Canada, preaching his message and gaining credibility and followers. In 1905, he traveled to Texas, where he established another bible school. Among the students who attended the new school was William J. Seymour, a young black preacher who was active in the Holiness movement. Seymour embraced Parham's ideas and soon afterward moved to Los Angeles to pastor a Baptist church. After just a few Holiness sermons, Seymour was removed from his position. Undeterred, he opened his own ministry, which shortly grew too large for the home in which he was living. As he preached, more and more members of his congregation began to experience the gift of tongues and on April 12, 1906 Seymour himself claimed to have received the gift. The rapid expansion of the congregation made it necessary to look for a larger meeting space, and the group decided on the former Stevens African Methodist Episcopal Church at 312 Azusa Street as the new gathering place.

Very soon after the new Azusa Street space opened, the Los Angeles *Times* writer described the scene:

> Breathing strange utterances and mouthing a creed which it would seem no sane mortal could understand, the newest religious sect has started in Los Angeles. Meetings are held in a tumble-down [sic] shack on Azusa Street . . . and the devotees of the weird doctrine practice the most fanatical rites, preach the wildest theories and work themselves into a state of mad excitement in their peculiar zeal.

> Colored people and a sprinkling of whites compose the congregation, and night is made hideous in the neighborhood by the howlings of the worshipers, who spend hours swaying forth and back in a nerve-racking attitude of prayer and supplication. They claim to have "the gift of tongues," and to be able to comprehend the babel.
> Then it is that pandemonium breaks loose, and the bounds of reason are passed by those who are "filled with the spirit," whatever that may be.[13]

Clearly the reporter viewed the congregation's activities with a skeptical eye, as did many others. Nevertheless, the small congregation began to draw converts and the Azusa Street Revival ultimately came to be seen by religious historians as the starting point for the Pentecostal movement in the United States.[14]

An interesting fact about the early movement is that it was interracial at a time in United States history when racial mixing was uncommon and indeed dangerous in many places. William Seymour was the son of slaves--a man who had very little formal education and who was not trained in public speaking or in social skills. However, he was so inflamed with his passionate conviction of the power of the Spirit that he was able to attract many who desired the sanctification he described, and the interracial ideals that were embraced by his congregation began to be emulated in other Pentecostal groups.

By 1910, the ideals of interracial worship and fellowship became a primary social as well as a theological issue for Pentecostals. The Church of God in Christ (COGIC), a prominent African-American Holiness church, began to invite white fellowships into the fold. The Pentecostal Assemblies of the World (PAW) also made efforts to absorb whites who had defected from mainline churches.[15]

These generous gestures were not bilateral. White Pentecostals, even when agreeing with the interracial vision in theory, proved to be unable to implement the principles in practice. Racism and Social Darwinism crippled the attempts of white leaders to make room for blacks in their congregations, especially in the American South, where racial mixing was illegal. Ultimately, many white Pentecostals came together to form the predominantly white United Pentecostal Church.[16]

In spite of this reality, the black Pentecostals held to the interracial ideal. In 1918, The Church of God in Christ published a statement in its church manual that read, in part, "The Church of God in Christ recognizes the fact that all believers are one in Christ Jesus and all its members have equal rights. Its overseers, both colored and white, have equal power and authority in the church."[17]

Even though racial segregation has continued to plague the Pentecostal vision, the ideal of egalitarian worship persists. It embraces not only racial equality but also equality between the sexes, and it remains an indicator of the widespread appeal of Pentecostal values, not only in the United States, but worldwide.

THE ROLE OF WOMEN

In Los Angeles, a young woman stood before a crowd of 5,000 worshippers, promising "food for the hungry, strength for the faint, hope for the hopeless, and sight for the blind" if only they would let Christ heal them.[18]

From its earliest days, the Holiness movement had welcomed women into its preaching ranks. Maria Beulah Woodworth-Etter was a Holiness preacher whose heyday preceded the Pentecostal movement by several years. She would conduct her meetings standing perfectly still with her hands in the air while the congregation would shout, weep, or fall into trances for hours at a time.[19]

The mission statement of Charles Fox Parham's Bethel Bible College, established in 1900, stated as its purpose, "to fit men and women to go to the ends of the earth to preach." The Azusa Street Mission counted many women among its members, not only as congregants, but also as pastors and missionaries. In 1913 at least 84 of the 361 Church of God in Christ ministers were women.[20]

Into this favorable environment entered Aimee Semple McPherson, one of the most influential Pentecostal voices of the 20th Century. She was born in October 1890 to Methodist parents in Canada. During her teens, she embraced the Pentecostal spirit, and at the age of 17 she married Robert Semple, her Pentecostal preacher. The couple traveled to Hong Kong as missionaries, where Robert died two years later.

After returning to the States, Aimee continued her ministry. While working in New York, she met Harold McPherson and the two were married in 1912. McPherson accompanied his wife on her evangelizing mission for a short time, but the marriage did not last. In 1918, after her husband filed for divorce, Aimee moved to Los Angeles, where her meetings became increasingly popular. She was praised for her speaking skills, and she became a darling of the Los Angeles press. In 1917, Aimee created *The Bridal Call,* a monthly magazine dedicated to spreading the message of the Spirit, and she began to attract a sizeable number of followers. She also began to attract favorable attention from the press.[21] By 1923 she had accumulated enough capital and enough followers to open the Angelus Temple, which could hold up to 5,300 worshippers. In 1924, the Angelus Temple radio station was created and in 1925 the Angelus Temple Bible School moved into its own building.[22]

Aimee Semple McPherson became a star personality, and her movements were the subject of keen popular interest. Her public sermons were advertised and she made use of parades, uniforms, music and programs for all ages in order to attract people to her social action programs such as feeding the hungry.[23] Her career as a preacher was remarkably successful. At the height of her popularity, in 1926, Aimee suddenly disappeared without a trace. It was announced at the end of the May 26 service at the Angelus Temple that she had gone swimming at the beach in Santa Monica and not returned. A massive search began, and two searchers died in the effort. It was presumed that she had drowned, and a memorial service was held for her on June 20 amid a great public outpouring of grief.

On June 23, Aimee suddenly turned up unharmed in Douglas, Arizona, where she said that she had been kidnapped from the beach and held in a remote cabin. Her return was wildly celebrated, and she was welcomed back to the Angelus Temple by 150,000 people.[24] Inconsistencies in Aimee's kidnapping story brought about further investigation and she was accused of lying and of faking her own death amid much speculation concerning possible motives. Despite the controversy, and despite charges of obstruction of justice, the case against her was eventually dropped for lack of evidence, and she was able to remarry and to resume her ministry. She died in 1944 of an accidental prescription drug overdose, and thousands once again mourned her passing.

Although her career was plagued by controversy, Aimee Semple McPherson stands as one of the most influential Pentecostal preachers of the 20th Century. She, along with contemporary preacher Billy Sunday, understood the value of modern media in spreading the message of the Spirit as well as for raising funds for social action programs.

While Aimee Semple McPherson is perhaps one of the best-known female Pentecostal preachers, there were many other women who rose to leadership roles within the movement. Since the years of the Holiness movement a century earlier, women had been accepted not only as ordained preachers, but also in many cases as pastors, and healing had long been a specialty of many female Pentecostal preachers. During the 1890s the divine healing campaigns of feminist preacher Mary Woodworth-Etter were well attended throughout Florida, South Carolina, Indiana, Iowa, and Missouri, where people claimed to have been healed of such maladies as "cancer, tumor, heart disease, asthma, catarrh of bronchial tubes, rheumatism, and kidney trouble."[25]

In contrast to the policies of traditional mainline Christian churches, Pentecostal communities embraced the ministries of women, and by the middle of the 20th century had more women preachers than any other branch of Christianity.[26] Women, who had often been sidelined or even ignored in the mainline churches, enjoyed in the Pentecostal environment a degree of status and authority not often seen previously in ecclesiastical circles. The empowerment of traditionally marginalized social groups came to characterize the Pentecostal movement, and indeed, will have contributed to the spread of Pentecostalism far beyond the borders of the land of its birth.

GLOBAL EXPANSION

Azusa Street was not the only place in the world where the fire of the Holy Spirit appeared to be descending upon believers. In the British Isles and in other places, events were also taking place that would initiate a revival comparable to the one going on in the United States. In 1904, Evan Roberts, a junior preacher in Moriah Lougor in Wales, experienced what he called a "Baptism of the Spirit" which he said indicated his complete sanctification. He undertook a preaching mission in which he claimed that in order to be saved, one had to confess all sins, accept Christ publicly, eliminate all elements of sin in one's life, and commit to readiness to obey the Holy Spirit.[27]

In 1955, the Rev. M. P. Morgan, an eyewitness to one of Roberts' meetings, spoke with Aneirin Talfan Davies, a Welsh journalist, of his first encounter with Evan Roberts. He described himself as sitting and listening to another preacher, when suddenly,

> There was a noise as of one falling, and a whisper through the congregation. Mr. Morgan lifted his eyes to see what was the cause of the commotion, and there below he saw Evan Roberts, lying prostrate on the floor, with the perspiration bubbling from his brow—young women around him, wiping the sweat from his forehead.[28]

Evan Roberts had been praying out loud to the Spirit: "Bend me . . . Bend me!" He was rewarded with an experience of the Spirit that so overwhelmed him that he felt compelled to share his experience with anyone who would listen. Initially, he spoke of his experience to a small group of about 17 people, all of whom were moved by the Spirit. Within a week, however, his church was filled to capacity with people interested in hearing his story. By January 1905, the newspapers reported that 70,000 had been converted in less than three months.[29]

Also in 1905, in Pune, India, a lady named Pandita Ramabai, a Christian convert and missionary, began, with 30 women in her mission for widows, to pray daily for the help of the Holy Spirit in their ministry. On Thursday, June 29, the Spirit is said to have descended on the widows, enveloping them in flames and causing one of them to run for a bucket of water.[30]

In Pyong-Yang, Korea, at the 1907 New Year Bible Study course, which was attended by over 1,500 people, the "Spirit of prayer" broke out at one of the meetings, and participants began to weep and to pray out loud simultaneously. The Spirit, they claimed, went out with the participants to their home churches, and within the year 30,000 were reported to have been converted.[31]

Similar events occurred in Valparaiso, Chile in 1909, in the Belgian Congo, Africa in 1914, in Lowestoft, England in 1921, and in Gahini, Rwanda in 1936.[32] Thousands experienced the fire of the Spirit, embraced the gift of tongues, and began to preach the message. There is little or no evidential support to show, however, that any of the converts actually became able, in fact, to speak in a foreign language.

It is estimated that half the Pentecostals in the world are found in Latin America, which has historically been predominantly Catholic.[33] While many historians believe that Latin American Pentecostalism originated in the North American movement, Alan Anderson makes the claim that there were already several Pentecostal denominations in Latin America several years before the birth of the major Pentecostal denominations in the United States. If Anderson is correct, these branches of Latin American Pentecostalism would have developed quite independently of their North American counterparts.[34]

Chile was the first Latin American country to see the emergence of Pentecostalism. Willis Collins Hoover (1858-1936) was a North American Methodist minister who had arrived in Chile in 1889 and was pastor of Chile's largest Methodist congregation. Intrigued by the events that were reported on Pandita Ramabai's widows in Pune, India, Hoover and his congregation began to pray for the descent of the Holy Spirit in Chile. In April 1909, Hoover reported that his congregation had experienced the Spirit, and he described the behavior that accompanied the event: weeping, uncontrollable laughter, fainting, rolling on the floor, visions, and, of course, speaking in tongues.[35]

In spite of the hostile reaction of the local authorities and the Methodist Church, Hoover persisted in his conviction that the Spirit had sanctified his congregation, and he eventually left the mainline Methodist Church and renamed his church the *Iglesia Metodista Pentecostal* (Methodist Pentecostal Church). This became the first Pentecostal church in Latin American and it was in no way affiliated with the North American Methodist Church, although it did retain some of the practices of the church such as infant baptism. Currently, there are more than thirty Pentecostal denominations in Chile that have emerged from this original movement.

Besides Chile, Brazil's Pentecostal population is one of the largest in the world. Between 1990 and 1992, 91 percent of the 710 churches built in Brazil were Pentecostal. Only one church built during this period was Catholic.[36]

The Pentecostal movement was introduced to Brazil by an Italian-American, Luigi Francescon, a Waldensian, who had arrived in Saõ Paulo in 1910 to minister to the large Italian Presbyterian community there. After being removed from his mainline ministry for preaching the baptism of the Spirit, Francescon formed the first Pentecostal church in Brazil, the *Congregacioni Christiani*. It began to attract native Brazilians, and the congregation of what is now called the *Congregação Cristã* now numbers between 1.5 and 2 million.[37]

The largest Pentecostal congregation in Brazil is the *Assembléas de Deus* (Assemblies of God), which, in 2000, numbered between four and eight million members. This church was established by Gunnar Vingren and Daniel Berg, two missionaries from the Swedish Pentecostal Church in Chicago, who arrived in Brazil in 1910 and began to hold meetings in a Baptist church in Saõ Paulo. After earnest prayer, the two missionaries claimed to receive baptism in the Spirit, and with a sense of divine authorization, they created the Apostolic Faith Mission, later renamed the *Assembléa de Deus* (Assembly of God). At present, Saõ Paulo boasts over a thousand *Assembléa de Deus* congregations.[38]

In Africa, Pentecostalism and other Charismatic[39] movements have become the fastest-growing religious movements on the continent. But African Pentecostalism, present since 1907, has its own peculiar style. As in Pentecostal denominations everywhere in the world, one observes in Africa the usual incidences of fainting, weeping, and speaking in tongues. In addition, since the 1970s Africa has experienced a number of developments that further distinguish African Pentecostalism from Western versions. Ritual symbolism like the use of holy water and the wearing of distinctive robes or vestments, as well as a growing inclusion of African traditional culture set the African churches apart. Overall, however, Pentecostalism has enjoyed tremendous success in Africa.

In Asia, at least a third of the Christian population is Charismatic or Pentecostal, and the trend is steadily strengthening. Asia, Africa, Australia, and the Pacific together contain three quarters of the world's Pentecostal and Charismatic population. In the year 2000, an estimated 33 million Pentecostals and Charismatics lived in India and Sri Lanka.[40]

India, as indicated earlier, had already seen the emergence of Pentecostalism in the mission house of Pandita Ramabai in 1905-1907. In Thailand, Pentecostal ideas were introduced by Finnish Pentecostal missionaries Hanna and Verner Raassina in 1946. It is Indonesia, however, that has seen the greatest degree of Pentecostal growth. A predominantly Muslim country, Indonesia is home to between 9 and 12 million Pentecostals and Catholic Charismatics, or 4-5 percent of the population. Pentecostalism came to Indonesia in 1964, when a Rote Island preacher, Johannes Ratuwalu, arrived in East Timor to conduct healing services. As word spread of the many healings that occurred, a Pentecostal revival was inaugurated that soon expanded throughout the island.

PENTECOSTALISM AND EMPOWERMENT

It is clear that Pentecostalism is a vibrant global phenomenon; within a century of its appearance, it has expanded to almost every country in the world. But why has it enjoyed such an amazingly rapid growth and acceptance, especially among countries in the developing world? A writer in *Christian History Magazine* explains that:

> Though most early Pentecostals [in the United States] came out of the blue-collar working class, the movement thrived among the poor and marginalized of society. Early Pentecostals taught a "theology of the poor," interpreting their remarkable growth as God's special favor upon the poor.[41]

Harvey Cox agrees that it was the "down and out" who were most receptive to the message. He writes that the fire of the Spirit spread among people whose lives were uncertain and who were looking for something greater than conventional religion and its perceived failure to deliver on its promises of hope for the poor.[42] If it was true in the United States that people were looking for something that would better benefit the poor, it is not difficult to imagine a similar effect on people in developing nations, whose lives under colonial rule certainly did not reflect the ideals presented in the Christianity of the ruling powers. It seems clear that Pentecostalism may have presented an opportunity to express local customs and values within a Christian context, although not necessarily the Christianity originally presented by the missionaries. According to Allan Anderson,

> One of the reasons for the growth of Pentecostal and Charismatic churches [in Africa] may be that they have succeeded where western founded churches have often failed – to provide a contextualized Christianity in Africa. They are essentially of African origin (even when founded by western Pentecostal missionaries) and fulfill African aspirations, with roots in a marginalized and underprivileged society struggling to find dignity and identity in the face of brutal colonialism and oppression. In some parts of Africa, Pentecostalism expanded initially among people who were neglected, misunderstood and deprived of anything but token leadership by their white ecclesiastical "masters." But despite these important social and historical factors, fundamentally it is the ability of

African Pentecostalism to adapt to and fulfill religious aspirations that continues to be its main strength.[43]

While Anderson's ideas may explain the popularity of Pentecostalism in the developing world, even Europe, the center of Western secularism, has shown itself not to be exempt from the allure of the religion. In England, for example, between 1985 and 1990, Baptist, Methodist, Presbyterian, Anglican, and Roman Catholic churches all lost members, with the Catholics and the Anglicans suffering as much as a 10 percent loss. At the same time, according to Harvey Cox, "independent Christian churches," which include mainly Pentecostals and some neo-Charismatics,[44] showed an increase in membership of nearly 30 percent.[45] In some places in Europe, moreover, Pentecostalism seems to be gaining the most popularity among women. In Sicily, for example, two out of three Pentecostals are women. Harvey Cox sees this growth to be a result of women's finally coming into their own after centuries of living in a patriarchal society:

> Many of these women have become Pentecostals in defiance of the express prohibition of their fathers and husbands. In other words, by the sheer act of converting to this often despised and ridiculed faith, they have taken a risky and venturesome step against Sicilian patriarchal culture. They have disobeyed the men whose honor depends on controlling them, and in a manner which – because of its openly public character – was bound to bring shame and censure on those men.[46]

It would seem that the ideas of Cox and Anderson may also apply in the many other European countries where women have also been an historically oppressed group. Pentecostalism clearly offers women, at least in Sicily, but very probably in the rest of Europe as well, an opportunity to express a personal spirituality in defiance of the religion of the "oppressors" without having to forsake Christianity altogether.

It appears, then, that at least in some places, the trend toward Pentecostal and Charismatic spirituality shows a need much deeper than the promises of traditional religion or even secular culture have been able to fulfill. As scholars like Allan Anderson and Harvey Cox have shown, this growing need seems to be finding satisfaction in the relative freedom of expression offered by Pentecostal and Charismatic communities, especially among those who have historically been poor and disenfranchised, but who are now in a position to choose their forum for spiritual expression.

During the 1960s, the American post-World War II generation also felt a deep spiritual need that was unfulfilled by traditional religion or secular culture. While many turned to religious practices of other times and places, others looked deeper within their own traditions to try to find meaning and hope amid the disappointments and upheavals of the period. Among these were a few American Catholics who found themselves attracted to the Cursillo, a Spanish spiritual program designed to foster a deeper personal relationship with the Holy Spirit and the Christian community. As the Cursillo became popular in the United States, a few American veterans of the movement applied Cursillo techniques and practices to a small new group of Catholic spiritual seekers who had undergone a life-changing experience at a weekend spiritual retreat organized by a group of students and professors at Duquesne University. The Duquesne Weekend, which represents the birth of the CCR, and the relationship of the CCR with the Cursillo movement, are examined in the next chapter.

NOTES

1. "Weird Babel of Tongues," *Los Angeles Times,* 18 April 1906, pg. III.
2. Web site of the World Christian Database; (accessed 6 June 2008); available from: www.worldchristiandatabase.org; Internet.
3. *Spirit and Power: A 10-Country Survey of Pentecostals.* The Pew Forum on Religion and Public Life, October 2006: 1.
4. Philip Jenkins, *The Next Christendom: The Coming of Global Christianity* (New York: Oxford University Press, 2002), 7-8.
5. ". . . . All of them were filled with the Holy Spirit and began to speak in other tongues as the Spirit enabled them ."Acts, 2:4 NIV.
6. Harvey Cox, *Fire From Heaven: The Rise of Pentecostal Spirituality and the Reshaping of Religion in the Twenty-first Century* (Cambridge: DaCapo Press, 1995), 4.
7. Vinson Synan, *The Holiness-Pentecostal Tradition: Charismatic Movements in the Twentieth Century* (Grand Rapids: William B. Eerdmans Publishing Company, 1997), 19-21.
8. *Pentecost* comes from a Greek word meaning "fiftieth" and refers to the fiftieth day after the resurrection of Christ, when the Spirit descended upon the Apostles as described in Acts 2:1-4.
9. Ted Olsen, "American Pentecost: The Story behind the Azusa Street Revival, the Most Phenomenal Event of Twentieth-century Christianity," *Christian History* 58 (Vol. XVII, No. 2): 10.
10. "Fire" refers here to the tongues of flame that appeared over the heads of the apostles at the descent of the Holy Spirit. See Ted Olsen, "American Pentecost: The Story behind the Azusa Street Revival, the Most Phenomenal Event of Twentieth-century Christianity," *Christian History* 58 (Vol. XVII, No. 2): 11-12.
11. John P. Kildahl, in The Psychology of Speaking in Tongues (New York: Harper & Row, 1972), explains that glossolalia, or speaking in tongues, "has come to

denote the experience in which a person seemingly speaks a language he has never learned, or a series of sounds not known to be speech of any group on earth." He also quotes Webster's Third New International Dictionary's definition of glossolalia as "ecstatic speech that is usually unintelligible to hearers," and the unabridged Random House Dictionary's definition as "a prayer characterized chiefly by incomprehensible speech" (p. 11). Glossolalia is a phenomenon that predates Christianity and which historically is found in both religious and non-religious contexts. Modern Pentecostals and Catholic Charismatics seem generally to consider glossolalia to be the spontaneous uttering of prophecy in a language that is not of earth, but rather is of heavenly origin. Spontaneous speaking in earthly languages of which the speaker has no previous knowledge is termed xenolalia, from the Greek words for "foreign" and "tongue."

12. Olsen, *American Pentecost*, 12.
13. "Weird Babel of Tongues," *Los Angeles Times,* 18 April 1906, pg. II, 1.
14. Synan, *The Holiness-Pentecostal Tradition,* 83, 105.
15. David D. Daniels, "They Had a Dream," *Christian History* 58 (Vol. XVII, No. 2): 20.
16. Daniels, *They Had a Dream*, 20-21.
17. *Church manual of The Church of God in Christ*, 1918. Quoted in James R. Goff, *Portraits of a Generation: Early Pentecostal Leaders.* (University of Arkansas Press, 2002), 255.
18. Aimee Semple McPherson. Sermon: *The Great "I Am" or "I Was"?*; (accessed 6 June 2008); available from: http://victorynetwork.org/McPherson.html; Internet.
19. "Setting the Vision: Pentecostalism's Early Leaders," *Christian History* 58 (Vol. XVII, No. 2): 35.
20. David G. Roebuck, "Loose the Women," *Christian History* 58 (Vol. XVII, No. 2): 38.
21. Edith L. Blumhofer, "Sister," *Christian History* 58 (Vol. XVII, No. 2), 32.
22. Ibid., 33.
23. Ibid.
24. Ibid.
25. Synan, *The Holiness-Pentecostal Tradition,* 190-191.
26. Ibid.
27. The Revival Library (accessed 10 September 2008); available from: http://www.revival-library.org/index.html?http://www.revival-library.org/pensketches/robertse.htm
28. "The Day that Evan Roberts Started the Flame," *The Western Mail,* 10 March 1955; (accessed 8 June 2008); available from: http://www.welshrevival.org/newspapers/1955.03wm.htm Internet.
29. Selected and adapted from *Flashpoints of Revival;* (accessed 6 June 2008); available from: http://www.pastornet.net.au/renewal/fire/ff-1900.htm ; Internet.
30. Ibid.
31. Ibid.
32. Ibid.

33. Allan Anderson, *An Introduction to Pentecostalism* (Cambridge: Cambridge University Press, 2004), 279.

34. Ibid., 63-64.

35. Willis Collins Hoover, *History of the Pentecostal Revival in Chile* (Santiago, Chile: Imprenta Eben-Ezer, 2000) pp. 9, 18-20, 29-32, 36, 78-73. Quoted in Allan Anderson, *An Introduction to Pentecostalism* (Cambridge: Cambridge University Press, 2004), 64.

36. Anderson, *An Introduction to Pentecostalism,* 69.

37. Ibid., 70.

38. Ibid., 71.

39. The Pew Forum on Religion and Public Life defines *Pentecostals* as "Christians who belong to pentecostal denominations and churches, such as the Assemblies of God, the Church of God in Christ or the Universal Church of the Kingdom of God." *Charismatics* "are other Christians, including Catholics and mainline Protestants, but who *either* describe themselves as "charismatic Christians," OR "describe themselves as "Pentecostal Christians" (but do not belong to explicitly Pentecostal denominations) OR speak in tongues at least several times a year." Pentecostals are generally not members of mainline churches, but rather tend to belong to specifically Pentecostal denominations. Charismatics may be either Protestant or Catholic; and while they exhibit many of the same behavior as Pentecostals, they usually remain established within the mainline churches. *Neocharismatics* may not belong to any church, but generally they tend to belong to independent nondenominational groups such as the Vineyard Christian Fellowship.

There are theological as well as ecclesiastical differences between Pentecostals and Charismatics. Where Pentecostals place great emphasis on signs such as glossolalia as evidence of Baptism in the Spirit, Charismatics, while placing great value on visible charisms, may or may not subscribe to the necessity of such signs, and may instead simply recognize the presence and the work of the Spirit in their lives and in their churches, as this author has personally observed.

The ecclesiastical and theological differences between Pentecostals and Charismatics have resulted in tensions that persist in spite of attempts on the part of some members of both groups to establish a common identity as Christians. For example, Patti Gallagher Mansfield, a Catholic Charismatic, saw her early charismatic experiences in the interdenominational meetings at the home of Flo Dodge as holding the promise of increased ecumenical dialog, but this promise is still far from being realized.

40. Anderson, *An Introduction to Pentecostalism,* 123.

41. *Christian History* 58 (Vol. XVII, No. 2): 2-3.

42. Harvey Cox, *Fire From Heaven: The Rise of Pentecostal Spirituality and the Reshaping of Religion in the Twenty-first Century* (Cambridge: Da Capo Press, 1995), 67.

43. Anderson, *An Introduction to Pentecostalism,* 122.

44. *Neo-charismatics*, according to the *International Dictionary of Pentecostal and Charismatic Movements,* are "Christian bodies with Pentecostal-like experiences that have no traditional Pentecostal or charismatic denominational connections

(p. 928)." The *International Dictionary* also reports that Neocharismatics actually outnumber all Pentecostals and Charismatics combined, with a 2002 total of some 295 million as compared with 65 million Pentecostals and 175 million Charismatics (Catholic and Protestant combined) (p. 284).

  45. Cox, *Fire From Heaven,* 187.
  46. Ibid., 197.

Chapter Three

The Duquesne Weekend and the Cursillo Movement

THE CURSILLO MOVEMENT

Two of the leaders of the CCR, Steve Clark and Ralph Martin, were deeply influenced by their participation in a group of spiritual seekers that came to be known as the *Cursillo*[1] movement. The ideas and the methods employed by the Cursillo were later used in the CCR as well as in other denominations such as the Methodists (Emmaus Walk) and the Episcopal church (Episcopal Cursillo). The Cursillo movement is seminal to the development of the CCR.

The *Movimiento de Cursillos de Cristiandad* emerged in Mallorca, Spain during the 1940s. The term *cursillo* refers to a three-day "short course" designed to effect a profound spiritual renewal in those who participate.

The official history of the Cursillo movement put forth by the Canadian Cursillos asserts that in 1943, Eduardo Bonnín Aguiló, a Catholic lay Spaniard, attended a silent retreat organized by the Catholic Action Diocesan Council in Mallorca in preparation for a pilgrimage to the shrine of San Diego de Campostela. The week-long closed program included talks given by a priest, periods of prayer, meditation, music, and group study. The retreat was very successful and the Catholic Action Diocesan Council became interested in creating a similar, albeit shorter, retreat program for the spiritual renewal of Catholics in their daily lives and not only for pilgrimage. Bonnín was chosen to serve as one of the presenters for the new cursillo, and he helped to design a three-day program that took place in August 1944 at Cala Figuera, Mallorca. The shortened cursillo was so successful that it was repeated every year until the much-publicized pilgrimage was finally completed in August 1948.[2]

The Canadian Cursillo web site lists Eduardo Bonnín as the official founder of the movement. However, according to the *New International Dictionary of Pentecostal and Charismatic Movements*, Bishop Juan Hervas, who was initially disciplined by the church for his support of the movement, is named by the church as founder or cofounder.[3] In time, however, the nascent Cursillo movement was accepted into the church. In 1966, Pope Paul VI gave an address (*Christ, the Church, the Pope Are Counting on You*) that gave credibility to the Cursillo and was subsequently published by the movement.

The three-day cursillo retreat gained in popularity and it spread throughout Europe and to North America, where it arrived in the United States in 1957, introduced by Spanish pilots being trained in Texas.[4]

THE CURSILLO PROGRAM

The cursillo is a short program that often takes place over a weekend. During a three-day period, a participant listens to a series of talks, or *rollos,* which may be given by a priest or by a member of the laity, and which are designed to completely "roll over" the participant in such a way that the listener experiences psychological changes leading to a permanent spiritual transformation. The program is described in the movement's literature as the result of a process of trial and error, culminating in the achievement of a "fullness" on January 7, 1949.[5] Participants describe their purpose in entering the program:

We were seeking a channel through which people could see the clear essence of being a Christian, with the exact reality of Christ with the world of possibilities and the depth of commitment that is involved in baptism itself.[6]

The intention of the cursillo was "to make possible, for those who practiced it, the true living of their Baptism."[7] From the start, the movement saw itself as operating within the parameters of the hierarchical church:

> In truth, from the very beginning, the Cursillo was not so much a movement in the Church as a movement of the Church . . . All the riches of the Heart of Christ were given exclusively to the Church. Only the Church could truly give a cursillo within the actual, vital and life-giving reality of the prayer and sacrifice of many joined to the action of the few. These few, who are of the two basic vocations in the Church – priesthood and laity – try to translate and let shine through, in group reunion, the intimate and multiple reality of being Christian.[8]

The cursillo is divided into three basic stages: the *precursillo*, or preparatory period, the actual *cursillo*, or three-day intensive program, and the *postcursillo*, an ongoing transformational process in which the *cursillista*, or participant, continues to function as part of a Cursillo community that supports his or her continued spiritual growth and functioning.

The precursillo period is a time of soul searching and preparation for the participant. This preparatory period continues until the first evening of the three-day intensive program. The applicant is often invited to attend a Cursillo meeting by a member (cursillista), who answers any questions the aspirant may have and who introduces the person to the movement. If the aspirant expresses interest in participating in the three-day cursillo intensive weekend, the cursillista acts as a sponsor for the applicant. The sponsor's responsibilities include explaining the program clearly to the aspirant, ensuring that the application forms are completed and submitted correctly (sometimes the sponsor may assume responsibility for all or part of the program fees), and ensuring that the applicant has transportation to and from the weekend program. The sponsor also consults with the person's pastor and their family members in order to assuage any concerns they may have about the program.

In the meantime, the applicant engages in a period of prayer and contemplation in preparation for the intensive weekend. The sponsor remains available to the applicant throughout the preparatory period and ensures that any questions or lingering concerns are addressed, so that the participant may enter the weekend program fully prepared and ready for spiritual growth.

The weekend cursillo program itself involves a combination of talks and individual and group activities intended to intensify the spiritual experience of the participants. The talks comprise three basic themes, selected and organized for the greatest psychological impact. Bord and Faulkner describe these themes as follows:

> The first theme, or phase, is designed to be low-key with very little direct pressure. The goal at this stage is to attempt to reduce any resistance that may exist due to the participant's anxiety that someone is out to convert him or her. The second theme involves the generation of anxiety and self-doubt. At this stage the talks stress that whatever the Cursillista was prior to the Cursillo, he or she was woefully inadequate as a Christian. This is the beginning of the effort to "form" the Cursillista . . . Anxiety is also aroused by emphasizing the difficulty one will have living a Christian life once out of the Cursillo milieu. Secular society is depicted as a hostile environment; and it is at this point that the necessity for forming post-Cursillo support groups is presented to participants. The final theme concerns complete commitment to the Cursillo's goals, and emphasis is placed on activity which dramatizes and sustains that commitment.[9]

As the cursillo weekend progresses, participants form friendships within the group. The group reunion, during which participants share their experiences with each other after the weekend is over, provides a community base where the new cursillista can find support and encouragement during the postcursillo period.

Another characteristic of the cursillo weekend is the use of the "auxiliary." Participants in a cursillo weekend are often divided into small groups, and each group has an established cursillo leader, an "auxiliary," assigned to it. The auxiliary participates in the group activities as a regular participant and is not identified as a leader until the end of the program weekend. The auxiliary is charged with the responsibility of supporting the desired responses and behaviors from participants and of identifying any possible problems, or individuals who may need additional counseling or attention. The cursillistas are subjected to psychological pressure from both the group and the auxiliary to have or to create an experience of deep, permanent commitment to the goals of the cursillo.

In defending the use of psychological pressure in the cursillo, cursillista Steve Clark, one of the founding members of the CCR movement, wrote, "The strategy of the Cursillo is to take a man out of a situation in which the group pressure is strongly secular and put him in a situation in which the group pressure is Christian and in which he can experience a true Christian community."[10] The pressure on the participant to experience the desired result of the intensive program and to create ongoing relationships and commitment to the group has been present in the CCR since the Duquesne Weekend, which will be discussed below.

The third, or *postcursillo,* stage of the Cursillo program is also called *ultreya,* a Spanish word with Latin roots meaning "onward." Ultreya also refers to a regular postcursillo meeting (often a weekly meeting) that provides continuity and nurturing among cursillistas from various communities within a particular region.[11] One who participates in a cursillo weekend is thought to undergo a spiritual transformation that is expected to continue throughout one's life. Ralph Martin, another of the co-founders of the CCR, writes, "Right after I made a Cursillo when I was a senior at the university of Notre Dame, I began meeting in a small group with other men to help each other review how we were doing on our journey. I've been in such a group now for more than forty years, and it's been an important help for me and for millions of others as well."[12] In reminiscing about her experience of the Duquesne retreat, Elaine Kersting Ransil has written that "it just seemed the most obvious thing in the world to continue to meet together in prayer."[13] Patti Gallagher Mansfield, in her memoirs, notes that following the Duquesne Weekend, "we joined together in such ventures as the Antioch Weekend, a student oriented retreat program based on the Cursillo which was developed by our friends [Ralph Martin and Steve Clark] from Michigan."[14] Referring to the ongoing prayer group meetings in which Charismatics participate, Archbishop Paul Josef Cordes has written that:

Such prayer groups should be encouraged, recognizing the faithfulness with which many of them [Charismatics] have been meeting for years. They are a source of Christian edification, a stimulus for faith and prayer; they offer mutual support and are a form of apostolic witness. The members of these groups are often active in their parishes and in other Catholic organizations. Prayer groups have produced many vocations to the priesthood and religious life. This, too, is a sign that the Holy Spirit is at work through such groups for the good of the whole Church.[15]

The elements of a shared group experience, emphasis on the Holy Spirit, public testimony, and the creation of a reality based on continued identity with a community discovered or developed around the conversion experience are all found in the CCR, in which Steve Clark and Ralph Martin[16] were prominent early leaders. Both Clark and Martin were committed cursillistas and both achieved high positions in the Cursillo movement before becoming involved in the nascent CCR.[17]

THE DUQUESNE WEEKEND AND THE CASE OF PATTI GALLAGHER MANSFIELD

In a letter dated April 29, 1967, Patti Gallagher (now Mansfield) explained to her former French teacher her reasons for cancelling her anticipated summer visit to Europe. Patti, a French major who had been planning a career teaching French, had lost interest in spending the summer in France because, she wrote, she had experienced an event which she felt had changed her life in such a way that it was no longer her own, and she felt impelled instead to "put everything else aside and follow the Lord Jesus unconditionally."[18] Patti later described the event and her experience in detail in her book, *As By a New Pentecost*, in which she presents her personal recollections of the events surrounding this pivotal moment in her life.

Patti Gallagher Mansfield was a student at Duquesne University of the Holy Spirit in Pittsburgh, Pennsylvania, a Catholic institution established by members of the Congregation of the Holy Spirit (the Spiritans), an order of priests and brothers founded in France in 1703.[19] A novice and rather timid member of the *Chi Rho*[20] Society, who was attracted to the society but concerned that Chi Rho membership might mark her as "too religious,"[21] Patti was invited through Chi Rho to attend her first-ever spiritual retreat the weekend of February 17-19, 1967 at the Ark and the Dove, a spiritual retreat house outside Pittsburgh. Patti had been favorably impressed by the friendliness and the warm welcome offered to her by the Chi Rho members, and although she still harbored conflicting feelings, she decided to attend the retreat.[22] In preparation, she read Acts 1-4 and *The Cross and the Switchblade* by David Wilkerson and she was "deeply impressed"[23] by both readings.

On the first evening of the retreat, Patti was particularly moved by one of the faculty advisors, who seemed to her to be filled with peace and joy as he spoke about the Virgin Mary and her qualities of faith and prayerfulness. The meditation on Mary was followed by a communal Penance Service, in which all the members confessed their sins to God and to each other. Patti found herself spontaneously praying out loud, which caused her to shed tears of embarrassment over her emotional state. Yet, she was aware of a profound desire for "something deep and lasting to take place" in her during the retreat.[24]

The following morning, Saturday, Patti attended a talk on Acts 2, after which the participants broke up into small discussion groups. During the discussion period, Patti realized her need for conversion in order to have the experience she so desperately wanted. Among her notes from that Saturday morning are the following:

- You have to *co-operate,* be willing to surrender your life and every aspect of it to the Lord. The joy of receiving the Lord is your life given back. . . . increased a hundredfold.
- JESUS, BE REAL FOR ME (P. Mansfield's capitals)
- To turn over our free will is the greatest gift we can give to God.
- David's proposal: A renewal of our Confirmation as part of Sunday prayers.
- our advisor's question: Are you ready for what the Spirit may do to you?
- My response: I'M SCARED.
- Are we ready to be fools?[25]

During the meeting, it was proposed that the participants should ceremonially invite the Holy Spirit into their lives in ceremony renewing their Confirmation vows, but the suggestion received a lukewarm reception. However, Patti was very favorably impressed with the idea of renewing her Confirmation because she very much wanted to invite the Spirit into her life. After the meeting was over, Patti wrote, "I WANT A MIRACLE" on a sheet of paper, and posted it for display.[26]

On Saturday evening, February 18, 1967, there was a birthday party scheduled for some of the students, but there did not seem to be much interest. There was a plumbing problem that threatened to end the workshop early and send the students home; and, while a plumber worked on the pipes, several students had retired to the chapel to pray for the problem to be resolved. According to Patti, after the students finished praying, they found that the water was restored, and they interpreted this as a sign that God wanted them to stay to complete the weekend, and Patti herself has reflected on the symbolism of the flow of water that evening. In considering the idea that some people might have seen the church of the time as lacking the water of life, she writes, "The Duquesne Weekend was a dramatic illustration of this fresh outpouring of the Holy Spirit in today's Church."[27]

Patti proceeded upstairs to the chapel to call the students who were gathered there to the birthday party. Although she says that she did not go with the intention to pray, she entered the room and found herself kneeling before the Blessed Sacrament, which she fully believed to be the real presence of Jesus. She writes, "As I knelt there that night, my body literally trembled before His majesty and holiness. I was filled with awe in His presence. He was there . . . the King of Kings, the Lord of Lords, the Great God of the Universe!"[28] Patti offered a prayer completely surrendering herself and her life to God, and then unexpectedly found herself flat on her face, her hands burning, barefoot, lying prostrate before the tabernacle, absorbed in the experience of God's personal and unconditional love.[29] After some time, Patti rose and sought out the chaplain in order to tell him what had happened to her. The chaplain replied that David Mangan, the student who had proposed the renewal of Confirmation, had had an almost identical experience about an hour before. Patti invited two of the other students to return to the chapel with her, where the three knelt before the tabernacle and Patti prayed aloud for the gift that she had received to be bestowed upon the others as well.[30]

Gradually, several other students were drawn to the chapel, where they began to undergo experiences similar to Patti's. Some were so overcome by the fullness of God's love that they began to weep; others were filled with such joy that they began to laugh. Some, including Patti, felt a burning sensation in their arms and hands, and some felt a tingling in their tongues or a clicking in their throats.[31]

However, not everyone had a positive experience. While one of the professors was convinced that the students had been baptized in the Holy Spirit, one student felt so repelled by what she saw that she left the house. The next day, Sunday, the student was still distraught, and the theology professor suggested that Patti command the evil spirit that was disturbing the girl to depart. Patti did so, and she reports that immediately afterward, the girl felt "relieved, but bewildered."[32]

The next morning, Sunday, Patti awoke with her hands still burning and tingling, and she asked the theology professor what this meant. He replied that she needed to lay her hands on people and to pray. He pointed to Gina Scanlon, a *Chi Rho* member who was pregnant, and said to Patti, "Let's pray for her. We can get two for one."[33]

When Patti returned to school the following day, one of her classmates asked her why she appeared to be drunk. She explained that she *was* drunk, but drunk on "the intoxicating love of God." When Patti opened her Bible and began to read to him, the student became frightened. After Patti recounted the weekend's events to her roommate of three years, the girl refused to room with her for their senior year, and even phoned Patti's parents with concerns about Patti's mental stability.[34]

One of the concerns that Patti's friends brought up to her was their fear that Patti would leave the church and join a Pentecostal group. But Patti felt even closer to her church than she had before the retreat experience. She began to examine her copy of *The Documents of Vatican II* and to research any reference she could find to the Holy Spirit, charisms, and spiritual gifts, and she came away convinced that the council documents held nothing but encouragement with regard to her experience.

Patti felt no uncertainty regarding her Catholicism, but she and other participants in the Duquesne Weekend felt that the Spirit was working through both Protestants and Catholics in order to bring unity among the groups. Shortly after the Duquesne Weekend, one of the *Chi Rho* participants wrote a letter to some friends in which he affirmed that,

> This also puts us in an ecumenical atmosphere at its best. Most of our Friday evenings we go to a prayer meeting with Anglicans, Presbyterians, Methodists, Lutherans, and Pentecostals. And for three hours all denominational differences are annihilated, without compromising an inch on our Roman Catholicism . . . Never have I heard the Church of Rome prayed for with such fervor as I have at prayer meeting. And with such love . . . To summarize; a little group of Protestants have shown us what it really means to be Catholics. And more than that. The Spirit of God is mightily at work here.[35]

THE GIFTS

After the Duquesne experience was over, several of the participants began to notice that certain "messages" kept coming to them throughout the day. As they began to share these messages with each other, they came to see them as manifestations of the gift of prophecy. Patti Mansfield recorded several of these messages, which convey a sense of God's love, as well as exhortations to live a life of hope and trust. One message in particular stands out:

> I live in the depths of your being . . . It is I Who have been with you since the beginning of time . . . You are My own . . . Never fear, for you are continually in My presence . . . If only you would trust Me, you would see how simple life is moment by moment.[36]

Patti Mansfield did not pray in tongues during the Duquesne Weekend, although she asserts that several others did. Patti writes of her friend David Mangan, who she says began spontaneously to pray in "beautiful, flowing French," a language of which he had no knowledge, during a prayer meeting shortly after the Duquesne experience. Patti prayed that she also would receive the gift of tongues, and on March 13, 1967, she awoke to what she describes as "the sound of clicking" in her throat. She skipped class and went instead to the University chapel, where she was determined to remain until she prayed in tongues. She describes what happened next:

> The clicking became louder; my mouth stated to move and then I began to grunt. 'Oh no,' I thought, 'don't tell me the Lord is going to give me an ugly, guttural tongue after I majored in French because of the beauty of the language!' But I kept grunting away until finally I was singing in tongues, a lovely song which flowed from the depths of my being. It was a beautiful language, different from the tongue I pray in now. Although I didn't recognize the words, in my heart I knew I was singing the Magnificat – the very passage the lord had given me the night I was baptized in the Spirit.[37]

Members of the group also came to believe that they had received the gift of healing. Mansfield describes how, upon hearing that her dormitory housemother had been hospitalized with phlebitis, she became convinced that the woman would be healed if Patti went to the hospital, laid hands on her, and prayed for her. After some initial hesitation, Patti did indeed go to the hospital the next day, where she took the woman's right hand and then traced a cross on the woman's forehead. Patti was astounded, when, a few days later, she saw the housemother back at school, and she attributed the woman's quick healing to the prayers that she had added to the woman's hospital treatment.[38]

Patti also came to believe that the Spirit had begun to teach her directly, through Scripture. When faced with a question, she would open her Bible at random and miraculously come to a perfect answer. Because of her direct and personal relationship with the Spirit, she says, "I found it difficult to engage in theological speculation or theoretical questions with other students in theology class." She also developed what she thought of as a "prophetic sense" of God's plans for people and events.[39]

These and other events convinced the participants in the Duquesne Weekend that they had indeed been baptized in the Spirit and that they had, in addition, received the classical charisms, or gifts of the Spirit, described in the New Testament.[40] They were persuaded that the time was right for them to begin to spread the good news of the movement of the Spirit among Catholics.

Chapter Three

EARLY EVANGELIZATION

The participants in the Duquesne Weekend returned to school on Monday morning still reveling in the experiences of the retreat, and they immediately began to tell their friends and classmates about their encounters with the Spirit. As documented by Patti Mansfield, not everyone received the news gladly. We have already seen, for example, that, after hearing Patti's account of the weekend retreat, Patti's roommate ceased to room with her, and even contacted Patti's parents with concerns about her sanity.

Nevertheless, still filled with the feeling of having been baptized in the Spirit and trusting that the Spirit would lead them, the students persisted in their efforts to spread the good news and to reach out to as many people as possible. On March 5, 1967, Patti attended an interdenominational prayer meeting at the home of Pentecostal Flo Dodge, where she felt completely welcomed and accepted by the group, instead of being subjected to the historical Protestant-Catholic tensions and prejudices that she expected to find there. Patti was convinced that the Spirit was truly present among the Protestants and Catholics who were gathered together at the meeting. She was able to envision a truly united Christian community that could be achieved through this shared experience of the Spirit.[41]

A week or two later, two leaders of the Cursillo movement, Ralph Martin and Steve Clark, arrived at the campus to discuss their own experiences of having been baptized in the Spirit, and they invited Patti and her classmate Marybeth Mutmansky to join them in their ministry after graduation. Patti and Ralph struck up a friendship, and, while visiting their families in New Jersey a couple of weeks later, Patti and Ralph attended a prayer meeting in New York City with a group of students from Fordham University, where, at Ralph's urging, Patti shared her testimony with the students from Fordham.[42]

Shortly after Easter of 1967, the Rev. Harald Bredesen visited the Duquesne campus. Bredesen, a Lutheran who had been baptized in the Spirit in 1946, had spoken of his spiritual experiences to Dr. and Mrs. Norman Vincent Peale. He had also had contact with John Sherrill, the senior editor of the Christian magazine *Guideposts*, who in turn had sought out the Baptism in the Spirit for himself. Years earlier, Sherrill had been introduced by the Reverend Bredesen to street preacher David Wilkerson, and Sherrill helped Wilkerson to write the neo-Pentecostal classic *The Cross and the Switchblade* (1962). Sherrill himself published *They Speak with Other Tongues* (1966), another classic of the neo-Pentecostal movement.[43]

During his visit to the Duquesne campus, Bredesen spoke about his experiences of the Spirit, as well as on topics like personal prophecy. He also invited the Catholics to spend the summer in his Mount Vernon, New York church, spreading the news of the Spirit in a mission of street evangelization. Patti, who had been planning to spend the summer holidays in France, prayed for guidance and became convinced that she had been called to evangelize. She cancelled her trip to France and decided, along with her friend Marybeth Mutmansky, to spend part of the summer working with Ralph Martin's campus ministry at Michigan State University, and part of the summer at Harald Bredesen's First Reformed Church in Mount Vernon, New York, where Patti learned the art of evangelization as she watched and worked with Pastor Bredesen as he ministered to the youth of Mt. Vernon.[44]

Patti Gallagher Mansfield graduated from Duquesne University and, instead of teaching French as she had originally planned, she taught religion at Mercy High School in Farmington, Michigan, and worked in campus ministry at the University of Michigan in Ann Arbor. She later worked in campus ministry in New Orleans, Louisiana at Loyola University of the South, and since 1971 has been engaged full time in working for the Charismatic Renewal movement worldwide.

As has been shown, Patti and the other early Charismatics perceived themselves as true Catholics and members of the Roman Catholic Church. Although filled with ecumenical ideals, they saw their primary purpose as being the spiritual renewal of the Catholic church and they intended to continue to work within the church to facilitate what they saw as the work of the Spirit. In fact, Patti and the others found validation in church documents that had been produced as a result of the Second Vatican Council and which called for the Spirit to create a "new Pentecost" in order to renew the church. But did the question of a personal relationship with the Spirit and the manifestation of charisms conflict with church authority? What was the response of the church to the Renewal movement? This was a complex issue that deserves careful examination.

NOTES

1. When referring to the movement itself, *Cursillo* is capitalized here; when referring to the weekend program, it is not capitalized.

2. History of the Cursillo Movement at the web site of the Canadian Cursillos; (accessed 6 June 2008); available from http://cursillos.ca/en/histoire/h2-eduardo.htm; Internet.

3. Stanley M. Burgess, ed. *The New International Dictionary of Pentecostal and Charismatic Movements* (Grand Rapids: Zondervan, 2002), 567-568.

4. Richard J. Bord and Joseph E. Faulkner, *The Catholic Charismatics: The Anatomy of a Modern Religious Movement* (Pennsylvania State University, 1983), 61. See

also: Stanley M. Burgess, ed. *The New International Dictionary of Pentecostal and Charismatic Movements.* (Grand Rapids: Zondervan, 2002.) 566-567.

5. *The Cursillo Weekend.* An Official Publication of the National Secretariat. (Dallas: The National Cursillo Center), 1.

6. Ibid., 2.

7. Ibid., 3.

8. Ibid., 3-4.

9. Bord and Faulkner, *The Catholic Charismatics*, 62.

10. Quoted in Bord and Faulkner, *The Catholic Charismatics,* 66.

11. From the Francophone Cursillo Movement of Canada web site; (accessed 25 May 2008); available from: http://cursillos.ca/en/faq/f05-ultreya.htm; Internet.

12. Ralph Martin, *The Fulfillment of All Desire: A Guidebook for the Journey to God Based on the Wisdom of the Saints* (Steubenville: Emmaus Road Publishing, 2006), 333.

13. Mansfield, *As By a New Pentecost,* 106.

14. Ibid., 62.

15. Paul Josef Cordes, *Call to Holiness: Reflections on the Catholic Charismatic Renewal* (Collegeville: The Liturgical Press, 1997), 56.

16. According to his website, "Ralph Martin is the President of Renewal Ministries and the host of the weekly television program The Choices We Face. He is the author of several books on the Catholic Church and spirituality and audio albums on the teaching of the saints. He is the Director of Graduate Programs in The New Evangelization at Sacred Heart Seminary in Detroit. Ralph is also Assistant Professor of Theology at Sacred Heart Major Seminary in the Archdiocese of Detroit as well as Visiting Professor of Theology at Franciscan University of Steubenville." Available at: http://www.renewalministries.net/staff.php#amartin.

Ralph Martin is still an important CCR leader; he was a featured speaker at the CCR's 2007 40th anniversary annual conference in Steubenville, Ohio. As I had the opportunity to attend this conference, I was impressed with Mr. Martin's popularity among the participants and with his continued commitment to the Catholic Charismatic Renewal.

17. Bord and Faulkner, *The Catholic Charismatics,* 60.

18. Letter to Mr. Val Iacovantuno from Patti Gallagher, April 29, 2967. Quoted in Mansfield, *As By a New Pentecost,* 5.

19. *Spiritus est qui vivificate* (It is the Spirit who gives life) is the motto of Duquesne University. (http://www.mission.duq.edu/index.html)

20. *Chi Rho* stands for the first two letters (chi=ch and rho=r) in the Greek word for "Christ." The *Chi Rho* has been used in cruciform as a symbol for Christ at least since the days of Constantine.

21. Mansfield, *As By a New Pentecost,* 33.

22. Ibid., 34.

23. Ibid.

24. Ibid., 36.

25. Ibid., 36-37.

26. Ibid., 38.

27. Ibid.
28. Ibid., 39.
29. Ibid., 39-40, 43.
30. Ibid., 40-41.
31. Ibid., 41.
32. Ibid., 41-42.
33. Ibid., 46.
34. Ibid., 47.
35. Ibid., 26.
36. Ibid., 49.
37. Mansfield, *As By a New Pentecost,* 50-51.
38. Ibid., 51-52.
39. Ibid., 53.
40. This author has personally observed experiences and behaviors similar to those described by Patti Mansfield and other participants at the Duquesne Weekend at non-Christian spiritual gatherings. Specifically, at Siddha Yoga meditation intensives between the years 1987 and 2004, this author witnessed participants speaking in tongues, barking like dogs, howling, sobbing, uncontrollable laughing, and fainting during extended chanting or meditation sessions. Also, participants in these sessions described sensations of heat, explosions of energy in the body, particularly in the spine and the top of the head, vibrations in the area of the spine and the forehead, and tingling in the hands and feet. These experiences were described as resulting in a feeling of enhanced well being, of personal expansion, or of unconditional love, and all was perceived as divine in origin. The author has also witnessed similar behaviors at the New York City Baha'i Center and at *satsangs* (spiritual gatherings) of devotees of Yogi Hari's Kundalini Yoga. Speaking in tongues is also an important element in *latihan*, the central spiritual practice of *Subud,* a 20th-century spiritual movement of Indonesian origin. In all cases there is a general group approval of such experiences; in fact, among the Catholic Charismatics at the June 2007 annual National CCR Conference at Franciscan University in Steubenville, Ohio , there seemed, in the author's opinion, to be a subtle pressure to experience speaking in tongues as a sign of truly having been baptized in the Spirit.
41. Mansfield, *As By a New Pentecost,* 53.
42. Ibid., 54.
43. Ibid., 55.
44. Ibid., 58-60.

Chapter Four

The Catholic Charismatic Renewal and Its Relationship with the Church, the Papacy, and Vatican II

BACKGROUND: THE MOOD PRECEDING VATICAN II

On January 25, 1959, the newly elected Pope John XXIII surprised the church with the announcement of his intention to convene an ecumenical[1] council. The First Vatican Council had taken place from December 8, 1869 - October 20, 1870 and had been summoned by Pope Pius IX for the purpose of addressing issues such as rationalism, liberalism, materialism, inspiration of Scripture, and papal infallibility. That council actually produced only two constitutions: the *Dogmatic Constitution On The Catholic Faith*, which addressed issues of faith and reason, and the *First Dogmatic Constitution on the Church of Christ*, which dealt with the primacy and infallibility of the bishop of Rome.[2]

During the period just preceding the First Vatican Council through the middle of the 20th Century, there developed an increasingly hostile relationship between the church and the modern world. Documents such as Pope Pius IX's 1864 *Syllabus of Errors* and the Pius XII's *Humani Generis* of 1950 condemned what was seen as the threat of modernity with all its secular values and emphases. The church resisted change and appeared to be trying to preserve traditional values and teachings in the face of scientific and technological progress that seemed to threaten the value of religion. The 20th century saw remarkable economic, political, and social changes and technological advances, and Pope John XXIII desired to bring the church into step with the modern world. His call for *Aggiornamento* (updating) reflected the Pope's vision for a church that more effectively addressed the needs of the faithful in the modern age. John O'Malley, a noted expert on Vatican II, has written:

Of all the affective needs felt by Catholics at the time the Council opened in 1962, few were more urgent among Europeans and Americans than the recognition that the Catholic cultural ghetto had to be terminated and a new attitude towards the "world" had to be assumed.[3]

O'Malley further explains that the council, which "consistently described *aggiornamento* in terms of adjustment or accommodation," continued Pope John's program by evaluating the world in a positive and optimistic way.[4]

VATICAN II: KEY DOCUMENTS AND IDEAS IMPACTING THE CCR

The Second Vatican Council (1962-1965) was an important event not only in the history of the Catholic church, but also in the emergence and early development of the CCR. The ideas and teachings that emerged from that council created sweeping changes in Catholic thought and practice. In his prayer to the Holy Spirit at the opening of the council, Pope John XXIII called upon the Spirit to "renew your wonders in our time, as though for [by] a new Pentecost."[5] The image of a "new Pentecost" came to be associated with the council and later with the CCR movement, which understood itself to be the manifestation of the Pentecostal work of the Spirit in the Catholic Church in modern times. Thomas Hughson, S. J., explains,

> The prayer and the phrase asserted more than "an enduring belief that the Holy Spirit would guide the deliberations of general councils," and more than belief that the Spirit who descended on Pentecost continues to indwell, unify, and sanctify the church. Taking those beliefs for granted, the prayerful phrase went on to join appeal to the Pentecostal event shortly after Jesus' death and resurrection with anticipation of something eventful in the sixth decade of the 20th century.[6]

CALL TO THE SPIRIT

In an effort to respond to the rapidly occurring changes in the world during the years following World War II, Pope John XXIII called for the updating (*aggiornamento*) of the church and its relationship with the faithful. The Second Vatican Council was summoned in order to revitalize and rejuvenate a church that appeared to be increasingly out of step with the modern world. One of the most important themes of the council was self-renewal, a "call to holiness" that would apply not only to the church itself, but to each and every member of the church. To this end, the Pope invoked the guidance of the Holy Spirit and expressed the hope that the council might become a "new Pentecost."[7] This receptivity to the work of the Holy Spirit also became a central characteristic of the CCR, which saw itself as a natural manifestation of the Spirit working in the world through individuals.

The council also worked to restructure the power relations in the church and to increase the decision-making power of the bishops. Richard Bord and Joseph Faulker, authors of *The Catholic Charismatics: The Anatomy of a Modern Religious Movement,* explain that "the document entitled 'Lumen Gentium' depicted authority in terms of service rather than of domination. It was designed to democratize the church."[8] Furthermore, the council also increased lay participation in church matters, and in reviving the role of the diaconate in church affairs, it made it available to married men, opening the way to a significant increase in lay participation in ecclesial activities.[9]

One of the most important elements that would have a particularly strong impact on the emergence of the CCR was the new spirit of openness and humility that allowed the church to accept ideas and recommendations from the laity. Also, key documents issued during the course of the council would not only inspire some Catholics, but would also be seen by them as encouragement of their newfound relationship with the Holy Spirit and the corresponding gifts that they sought and felt that they received. For example, paragraph 12 of *Lumen Gentium* (Dogmatic Constitution on the Church–1964), discussed below, has been called the *Magna Carta* of the Catholic Charismatic Renewal.[10] Paragraph 3 of the 1965 document *Apostolican Actuositam* (Degree on the Apostolate of the Laity) reiterated and reinforced the idea put forth in *Lumen Gentium* that the "holy people of God" play an important role in "Christ's prophetic office."[11] The idea that the laity had a role to play in the work of the Spirit of Christ became a seminal one in the emergence of the CCR. Later papal documents like Pope John Paul II's 1986 encyclical *Dominum et Vivificantem* (On the Holy Spirit in the Life of the Church and World)[12] and his *Christifideles Laici* (Apostolic Constitution: On the Vocation and Mission of the Lay Faithful in the Church and in the World–1988)[13] provided additional statements of papal support for the CCR and the gifts of the Spirit.

According to Bord and Faulkner, the objective of the CCR is "to bring as many people as possible to an experiential relationship with Christ."[14] In spite of the obvious potential for schism inherent in such a powerful enthusiastic movement, it has never been the intention of the CCR to separate itself from the church.

After Patti Mansfield's experience during the Duquesne Weekend, a friend expressed to Patti her fear that Patti and the others might leave the church. On this concern, Patti wrote, "I felt that I was discovering the Church in a wonderful new way . . . I said to myself, 'As intense as my experience of the Holy Spirit on the Weekend was, if the Church tells me this is not authentic, I would rather renounce my own experience than ever leave the Catholic Church.'"[15] Patti went home after the weekend retreat and immediately began to scour the council documents for anything that might be brought to bear on her experience. She writes that she found "nothing but encouragement" in the council documents; in fact, she says that she "rejoiced" as she read the following passage from *Lumen Gentium,* Article 12 (the emphasis is hers):

> The holy People of God shares also in Christ's prophetic office. It spreads abroad a living witness to Him especially by means of a life of faith and charity and by offering to God *a sacrifice of praise*, the tribute of lips which give honor to His name.[16]

Patti thought that this statement confirmed the verbal praise of God that manifested itself during her experience of having been "baptized in the Spirit." The "gifts of the Spirit" that Patti and the other participants believed they had received seemed also to be validated in the same document:

> It is not only through the sacraments and Church ministries that the same Holy Spirit sanctifies and leads the People of God and enriches it with virtues. Allotting His gifts "to everyone according as He will" (1 Cor. 12:11), *He distributes special graces among the faithful of every rank.* By these gifts He makes them fit and ready to undertake the various tasks or offices advantageous for the renewal and upbuilding of the Church, according to the words of the Apostle: " The manifestation of the Spirit is given to everyone for profit" (1 Cor. 12:7). These charismatic gifts, whether they're the most outstanding or the most simple and widely diffused, are to be received with thanksgiving and consolation for they are exceedingly suitable and useful for the needs of the Church.[17]

Patti explains her response to reading the Vatican II documents:

> The Church was clearly telling me through the Documents of Vatican II that my experience of the Holy Spirit was valid, even if certain individuals were looking at me askance. *What a relief to know that I could be both Catholic and Charismatic.* No choice had to be made. I later discovered that it was Cardinal Suenens whose intervention at the Vatican Council made these statements on the charisms so explicit.[18]

Cardinal Leon Joseph Suenens of Belgium was a progressive voice in the church. He had expressed a belief in the possibility of scientifically perfecting a morally acceptable birth control pill. During the council he had demonstrated a willingness to accept a "more open and flexible" relationship with atheists, and he had shown resistance to the papal ban on formal discussion of clerical celibacy. He was also known for his longtime support of allowing the laity to shoulder more responsibility within the church.[19] In him, the CCR found the support it required in order to remain a valid Catholic movement within the institutional church. Cardinal Suenens not only participated in the movement, but he also acted as liaison between the movement and the Vatican, and he published several works in support of the CCR.[20] Cardinal Suenens had long been interested in fostering a more democratic decision-making process within the church, and he had also concerned himself with the limits of papal authority. Thus, the shared responsibility implied in the idea of baptism in the Spirit seemed congruent with the Cardinal's thinking and with long-established goals.[21] Suenens had spoken of the importance of charismatic gifts during the Second Vatican Council and before the emergence of the CCR. In response to accusations that the CCR had manipulated the Cardinal's interest,[22] Suenens said, "I did not discover the Holy Spirit through the renewal. As I have said, the Spirit had long been at the center of my life."[23]

The Cardinal saw in the Renewal movement a "spiritual youth" and "a more tangible hope, and the joy of seeing impossible things become possible."[24] He evidenced a belief that the movement represented a revitalizing energy that could be used to the benefit of the church. The Cardinal was also acutely aware of the divisive potential of the movement and he took pains to see the movement firmly established within the church. This resulted in a gradual redirecting of the CCR's focus from an ecumenical one to a stronger Catholic identity in order to avoid any possible accusations of heterodoxy. To those who saw the Renewal as a splinter group, the Cardinal wrote, "Is the renewal some sort of injection of new blood into the body of Christ, something coming from outside? No. There is no such thing as an institutional church in contrast to a charismatic church. There is only one church."[25] Here Suenens was addressing not only critics of the Renewal movement, but also the Charismatics themselves. The Cardinal recognized that it was crucial to prevent any potential threat to the unity of the church. Therefore, he saw to it that those who participated in the movement also recognized the unity and the authority of the institutional church. He insisted that, "It is of the utmost importance that the charismatic renewal maintain this sense of continuity and not create the impression that the renewal is coming out of the blue to start radically new things."[26]

The leaders of the Renewal movement agreed wholeheartedly with the Cardinal, and they made efforts to strengthen their relationship with the Cardinal, with the institutional church, and especially with the Pope. Ralph Martin, one of the participants in the Duquesne Weekend and a co-founder of the movement, met with Pope Paul VI in Rome on October 10, 1973. Although the meeting was positive, the Pope's statement to Martin was carefully worded:

> We rejoice with you, dear friends, at the renewal of spiritual life manifested in the Church today, in different forms and in various environments . . . The spiritual lives of the faithful . . . come under the active pastoral responsibility of each bishop in his own diocese. It is particularly opportune to recall this in the presence of these ferments of renewal which arouse so many hopes.
>
> Even in the best experiences of renewal, moreover, weeds may be found among the good seed. So a work of discernment is indispensable . . . [and this discernment is the responsibility of] . . . those who are in charge of the Church.[27]

This statement was a clear caution to the leaders of the Renewal to remain mindful of the authority of the church on matters of the Spirit. The point was well taken, and Martin and his entourage returned to the United States encouraged by a feeling of having been accepted by the church at the highest levels. Although the Renewal had begun as, and remained, primarily a lay movement, clerical acceptance and participation were welcomed, and clerical participation in the movement began to increase. By 1975, as the result of the combined efforts of the CCR and its highest-ranking supporter, Cardinal Suenens, the CCR was formally acknowledged by the American bishops, and official liaisons between the bishops and the CCR were established.[28]

PAPAL RESPONSES TO THE CCR

As indicated above in Pope Paul VI's statement to the leaders of the Renewal movement in October, 1973, papal responses to the CCR have been positive but cautionary. In May, 1975, Pope Paul VI spoke to the International Conference on the Catholic Charismatic Renewal in Rome, where there were over 10,000 Charismatics attending. He said:

> Nothing is more necessary to this more and more secularized world than the witness of the "spiritual renewal" that we see the Holy Spirit evoking in the most diverse regions and milieu... How then could this "spiritual renewal" not be a "chance" for the Church and for the world? And how, in this case, could one not take all the means to insure that it remains so?[29]

Speaking to a group of international leaders of the Renewal on December 11, 1979, Pope John Paul II said, "I am convinced that this movement is a very important component of the entire renewal of the Church . . . Remain in an attitude of constant and grateful availability for every gift that the Spirit wishes to pour into your hearts." Noting that since age 11 he had said a daily prayer to the Holy Spirit, he added, "This was my own spiritual initiation, so I can understand all these Charisms. They are all part of the richness of the Lord. I am convinced that this movement is a sign of his action."[30]

John Paul II met with Charismatics and Charismatic leaders on many occasions during his long tenure as pontiff, and his relationship with the movement was congenial and supportive. He affirmed the work of the Spirit in the movement repeatedly, as in a private audience of 1979:

I am convinced that this movement is a sign of His action [of the Spirit]. The world is much in need of this action of the Holy Spirit, and it needs many instruments for this action . . . Now I see this movement, this activity everywhere.[31]

However, John Paul II also was careful to remind the CCR of its place within the church. In 1984, at the CCR's Fifth International Leaders' Conference in Rome, he said:

I ask you, and all the members of the Charismatic Renewal, to continue to cry aloud to the world with me: "Open the doors to the Redeemer." The church's mission is to proclaim Christ to the world. You share effectively in this mission insofar as your groups and communities are rooted in the local churches, in your dioceses and parishes.[32]

The pope was even more explicit about the position of the CCR within the church in his statement of March 14, 2002 to the participants in the National Congress of the Italian "Renewal in the Spirit":

> Yes! The Renewal in the Spirit can be considered a special gift of the Holy Spirit to the Church in our time. Born in the Church and for the Church, your movement is one in which, following the light of the Gospel, the members experience the living encounter with Jesus, fidelity to God in personal and community prayer, confident listening to his Word and a vital rediscovery of the Sacraments, not to mention courage in trials and hope in hardship. Love for the Church and submission to her Magisterium, in the process of maturing in the Church supported by a solid permanent formation are relevant signs of your intention to avoid the risk of favouring, unwittingly, a purely emotional experience of the divine, an excessive pursuit of the "extraordinary" and a private withdrawal that may shrink from apostolic outreach.[33]

The current pontiff, Benedict XVI, continues to maintain the position of cautious embrace established by his predecessors. In addressing pilgrimage participants in Rome on March 24, 2007, the Pope quoted John Paul II as saying that:

There is no conflict or opposition in the Church between the institutional and the charismatic dimensions, of which the Movements are a significant expression. Both are co-essential to the divine constitution of the People of God. In the Church the essential institutions are also charismatic and indeed the charisms must, in one way or another, be institutionalized to have coherency and continuity.[34]

Pope Benedict XVI also reminded the participants that:

Both dimensions originate from the same Holy Spirit for the same Body of Christ, and together they concur to make present the mystery and the salvific work of Christ in the world.

This explains the attention with which the Pope and the Pastors look upon the richness of the charismatic gifts in the contemporary age. In this regard, during a recent meeting with the clergy and the parish priests of Rome, recalling the invitation that St. Paul addressed in the First Letter to the Thessalonians not to extinguish the charisms, I said that if the Lord gives us new gifts, we must be grateful, even if sometimes they may be uncomfortable. At the same time, since the Church is one, if the Movements are really gifts of the Holy Spirit, they must, naturally, be inserted into the Ecclesial Community and serve it so that, in patient dialogue with the Pastors, they can be elements in the construction of the Church of today and tomorrow.[35]

Here the Pope clearly locates both the charisms and the CCR itself firmly within the arms of the church, stating that, while the charisms need to be accepted with respect and gratitude, it must also be recognized that they are intended to be used in the service of the church.

The CCR began as a movement among lay Catholics who claimed to have experienced a spiritual event that they described as being "baptized in the Spirit." In contrast with the Protestant Pentecostals, whose experiences of baptism in the Spirit resulted in their leaving the mainline Protestant churches and forming splinter groups and new Protestant sects, the Catholics who had experienced the descent of the Spirit looked to the church and to the documents of the Second Vatican Council for validation and acceptance of their experience.

The Catholic church, aware of the divisions in the Protestant churches that had resulted from the mainline churches' rejection of those who claimed to have experienced rebirth in the Spirit, chose to view the emerging Catholic movement with more benevolence, if also with caution. Due to the personal involvement and the efforts of Cardinal Leon Joseph Suenens to act as liaison between the nascent movement and the Vatican, the CCR enjoyed acceptance and official recognition from the church, especially through the

Popes. This recognition was extended with caution. The church, mindful of the potential for schism, insisted that while the charisms, or gifts, of the Spirit were available to all, those charisms were intended to be used in the service of the church; the movement itself was subject to the authority of the church teaching authority at all times. The Catholic Charismatics fully accepted these conditions, and they proceeded to embark on a mission of spreading the Charismatic message among their local parishes, where, in spite of the church's official approval, their efforts did not always meet with acceptance.

The CCR has had its share of academic and episcopal opposition. One of its early and particularly harsh critics, Dr. J. Massyngberde Ford, Associate Professor of Theology at Notre Dame, accused the founders of the movement of deliberately manipulating the attention of Cardinal Suenens in order to secure his support.[36] Cardinal Miguel Garcia of Mazatlan, Mexico, described the Renewal as "the smoke of Satan that has infiltrated the Church," and he banned the Renewal from his diocese. The Archbishop of Durango, Antonio Lopez, also condemned the movement and charged it with "elitism, fundamentalism, Protestant contamination, charismania (excessive emphasis on spiritual gifts), paraclericalism, and authoritarianism. In 1977, he prohibited the practices of "clapping, 'rhythmic movement,' baptism in the Spirit, and all charismata."[37] However, these critics represent a minority among the church hierarchy. The official position of the church, as has been demonstrated, is one of acceptance, provided that the movement remains subject to church authority. Still, the scene "in the pews" does not always conform to the movement's official legitimate status.

In personal conversations with individual Catholic Charismatics,[38] I heard repeated complaints that their Charismatic prayer groups were being marginalized in their home parishes. Because of the Charismatic style of worship, which normally includes praying with arms outstretched, speaking in tongues, prayer healings, and sometimes being "slain in the Spirit" (where a person becomes overwhelmed by the Spirit and collapses in a swoon), it is often difficult for mainline Catholics to accept Charismatics and to worship side by side with them. This friction sometimes results in the establishment of separate Charismatic masses and prayer services, which often take place in church basements or on weekday evenings. The Charismatics believe that their message is being rejected by other parishioners. They, nevertheless, remain convinced that their message and their experience of the Spirit is the "true" or "apostolic" Catholicism, and some Charismatics even hold that their non-Charismatic fellow parishioners have strayed from the apostolic tradition. This attitude clearly is not very different from the views of Protestant Pentecostals. It also seems to convey a sense of "spiritual elitism" that has the ironic effect of creating divisions among those who would see themselves as members of "one holy, catholic, and apostolic Church."[39]

NOTES

1. "Ecumenical" refers to the involvement of the entire church. There have been a total of 21 ecumenical councils in church history. According to the International Dictionary of Pentecostal and Charismatic Movements, 8 ecumenical councils took place in the first millennium before the split between Eastern and Western Christianity; 10 were councils of the pre-Reformation Western church, and 3 of the post-Reformation Roman Catholic Church.

2. Web site of Eternal Word Television Network (EWTN); (accessed 6 June 2008); available from: http://www.ewtn.com/library/COUNCILS/V1.HTM#1; Internet.

3. John O'Malley, "Reform, Historical Consciousness, and Vatican II's Aggiornamento," *Theological Studies* 32 (1971) 573-601.

4. Ibid.

5. Pope John XXIII. *Prayer to the Holy Spirit* (1961): Divine Spirit, renew your wonders in our time, as though for a new Pentecost, and grant that the holy church, preserving unanimous and continuous prayer, together with Mary the Mother of Jesus, and also under the guidance of St. Peter, may increase the reign of the Divine Saviour, the reign of truth and justice, the reign of love and peace. Amen. (Accessed 6 June 2008); available from: http://www.dovcharismaticrenewal.org/cr_views.html; Internet.

6. Thomas Hughson, S. J., "Interpreting Vatican II: A New Pentecost." *Theological Studies* (March 2008).

7. Pope John XXIII, *Prayer to the Holy Spirit* (1961): Divine Spirit, renew your wonders in our time, as though for a new Pentecost, and grant that the holy church, preserving unanimous and continuous prayer, together with Mary the Mother of Jesus, and also under the guidance of St. Peter, may increase the reign of the Divine Saviour, the reign of truth and justice, the reign of love and peace. Amen. (Accessed 06/06/08); available from: http://www.dovcharismaticrenewal.org/cr_views.html; Internet.

8. Bord and Faulkner, *The Catholic Charismatics,* 68.

9. Ibid.

10. Paragraph 12 reads as follows: *The holy people of God shares also in Christ's prophetic office; it spreads abroad a living witness to Him, especially by means of a life of faith and charity and by offering to God a sacrifice of praise, the tribute of lips which give praise to His name.(110) The entire body of the faithful, anointed as they are by the Holy One,(111) cannot err in matters of belief. They manifest this special property by means of the whole peoples' supernatural discernment in matters of faith when "from the Bishops down to the last of the lay faithful" (8*) they show universal agreement in matters of faith and morals. That discernment in matters of faith is aroused and sustained by the Spirit of truth. It is exercised under*

the guidance of the sacred teaching authority, in faithful and respectful obedience to which the people of God accepts that which is not just the word of men but truly the word of God.(112) Through it, the people of God adheres unwaveringly to the faith given once and for all to the saints,(113) penetrates it more deeply with right thinking, and applies it more fully in its life. It is not only through the sacraments and the ministries of the Church that the Holy Spirit sanctifies and leads the people of God and enriches it with virtues, but, "allotting his gifts to everyone according as He wills,(114) He distributes special graces among the faithful of every rank. By these gifts He makes them fit and ready to undertake the various tasks and offices which contribute toward the renewal and building up of the Church, according to the words of the Apostle: "The manifestation of the Spirit is given to everyone for profit".(115) These charisms, whether they be the more outstanding or the more simple and widely diffused, are to be received with thanksgiving and consolation for they are perfectly suited to and useful for the needs of the Church. Extraordinary gifts are not to be sought after, nor are the fruits of apostolic labor to be presumptuously expected from their use; but judgment as to their genuinity and proper use belongs to those who are appointed leaders in the Church, to whose special competence it belongs, not indeed to extinguish the Spirit, but to test all things and hold fast to that which is good.

Web site of the Vatican Archives; (accessed 10 September 2008); available from: http://www.vatican.va/archive/hist_councils/ii_vatican_council/documents/vat-ii_const_19641121_lumen-gentium_en.html; Internet.

11. Web site of Eternal Word Television Network (EWTN); (accessed 15 August 2008); available from:: http://www.ewtn.com/library/COUNCILS/V2LAITY.HTM; Internet.

12. Web site of the Vatican; (access 15 August 2008); available from: http://www.vatican.va/holy_father/john_paul_ii/encyclicals/documents/hf_jp-ii_enc_18051986_dominum-et-vivificantem_en.html; Internet.

13. Web site of the Vatican; (accessed 15 August 2008); available from: http://www.vatican.va/holy_father/john_paul_ii/apost_exhortations/documents/hf_jp-ii_exh_30121988_christifideles-laici_en.html; Internet.

14. Bord and Faulkner, *The Catholic Charismatics,* 107.

15. Mansfield, *As By a New Pentecost,* 47-48.

16. Ibid.

17. Ibid., 48.

18. Ibid.

19. Bord and Faulkner, *The Catholic Charismatics,* 111.

20. Cardinal Suenens composed a series of six works cumulatively known as the "Malines Documents," (named after the ecumenical center in Malines, Belgium) in which he addressed issues relating to the Catholic Charismatic Renewal movement. They are: *Charismatic Renewal*, followed by *Ecumenism and Charismatic Renewal* (1978); *Charismatic Renewal and Social Action* (1979); *Renewal and the Powers of Darkness* (1982); *Le Culte du Moi et Foi Chretienne* (1985); and *Resting in the Spirit* (1986).

21. Bord and Faulkner, *The Catholic Charismatics*, 112.

22. J. Massyngberde Ford, Associate Professor of Theology at Notre Dame, has been a longtime critic of the CCR, and has implied that the CCR leadership had courted and manipulated the Cardinal in order to secure his support. See Richard J. Bord and Joseph E. Faulkner, *The Catholic Charismatics: The Anatomy of a Modern Religious Movement.* (Pennsylvania State University, 1983), 109.
23. Quoted in Richard J. Bord and Joseph E. Faulkner, *The Catholic Charismatics,* 112.
24. Quoted in Bord and Faulkner, *The Catholic Charismatics,* 112.
25. Bord and Faulkner, *The Catholic Charismatics,* 112-113.
26. Quoted in Bord and Faulkner, *The Catholic Charismatics,* 112.
27. Quoted in Bord and Faulkner, *The Catholic Charismatics,* 108-109.
28. Bord and Faulkner, *The Catholic Charismatics,* 109.
29. Web site of Charismatic J. Dominguez, M.D.; (accessed 6 June 2008); available from: http://www.religion-cults.com/spirit/charismatic.htm#Popes_Statements; Internet.
30. Ibid.
31. *Web page of the International Catholic Charismatic Renewal Services (accessed 6 June 2008); available from: http://www.iccrs.org/johnpaul_ii.htm; Internet.*
32. *Address of Pope John Paul II at the Fifth International Leaders' Conference, Rome, 30 April 1984; (accessed 6 June 2008); available from: http://www.iccrs.org/johnpaul_ii.htm; Internet.*
33. Address of Pope John Paul II to the participants in the national Congress of the Italian "Renewal in the Spirit", Rimini, 14 March 2002; (accessed 6 June 2008); available from: http://www.iccrs.org/johnpaul_ii.htm; Internet.
34. Address of Pope Benedict XVI to Communion and Liberation Pilgrimage Participants, St. Peter's Square, 14 March 2007; (accessed 6 June 2008); available from: http://www.fraternityofsaintcharles.org/publications.cfm?id=95; Internet.
35. Address of His Holiness Pope Benedict XVI to Communion and Liberation Pilgrimage Participants, St. Peter's Square, 14 March 2007; (accessed 6 June 2008); available from: http://www.fraternityofsaintcharles.org/publications.cfm?id=95; Internet.
36. Bord and Faulkner, *Catholic Charismatics,* 109.
37. Blancarte 1992, 359. Quoted in "A preferential option for the spirit: The Catholic charismatic renewal in Latin America's new religious economy." Latin American Politics and Society, Spring 2003 by Chesnut, R Andrew; (accessed 6 June 2008); available from: http://findarticles.com/p/articles/mi_qa4000/is_200304/ai_n9210859/pg_10; Internet.
38. From June 8-10, 2007, I attended the 40th Anniversary Catholic Charismatic Conference at the Franciscan University of Steubenville, the present home of the Catholic Charismatic Renewal in the United States. Among the speakers at the conference were Patti Gallagher Mansfield and Ralph Martin, two of the original participants at the Duquesne Weekend. During the conference, I had many opportunities to converse with other participants, and I made notes of my conversations.
39. From the Nicene Creed, the universal Catholic statement of belief that is recited at every Catholic Mass since the Council of Nicaea in 325 C.E.

Closing meal at Duquesne Weekend, February 1967.

Duquesne University.

Men from Chi Rho at a picnic prior to the Duquesne Weekend.

Students on the Duquesne Weekend doing dishes.

Living room at the Ark and the Dove Retreat House.

Patti Mansfield at the time of the Duquesne Weekend.

David Mangan and Patti Mansfield, 2009.

Chapter Five

Changes in the Charismatic Movement in the Late 20th Century

The CCR has evolved from a weekend retreat of about 25 college students in Pittsburgh, Pennsylvania in 1967[1] to a global phenomenon numbering over 119,910,000 in 235 countries by the beginning of the 21st Century.[2] The Pew Forum reports that in the United States in 2006, more than 3 in 10 Catholics could be classified as Charismatic. In Latin America and in Asia, the percentages are considerably higher.[3] The CCR has undergone significant changes in structure, demographics, and in its relationships with both the Catholic and the Protestant churches.

ECUMENISM AND CENTRALIZATION

The Duquesne Weekend was organized by four Catholic faculty members who had attended a series of interfaith prayer meetings led by a charismatic Presbyterian, Flo Dodge. Two of the professors presiding over the retreat, Ralph Keifer and Bill Storey, had been prayed over for baptism in the Holy Spirit at a meeting at Ms. Dodge's home that had taken place about a month previously.[4]

Even though only Catholics attended the Duquesne retreat in February, 1967, the early Catholic Charismatics worshiped freely with a mix of Catholics, Pentecostals, and Protestant charismatics, including the president of the local Protestant Full Gospel Business Men's Fellowship International (FGBMFI), Ray Bullard.[5] During the summer of 1967, just a few months after the Duquesne retreat, Patti Gallagher Mansfield spent several weeks living and working in the parsonage of the Rev. Harald Bredesen, Pastor of the First Reformed Church in Mt. Vernon, New York. The Rev. Bredesen had invited several of the Duquesne Catholics to spend the summer in his church for the purpose of gaining experience in "street evangelization."[6]

Although Patti Gallagher Mansfield and other Catholic Charismatics remained committed to the Catholic church and were determined to function within ecclesiastical parameters, they maintained a collegial relationship with the local Protestant charismatics, and the newly converted Catholics saw the work of the Spirit in ecumenical terms. Patti Mansfield tells how, after the Duquesne retreat, several of the participants continued to attend the mixed Catholic/Protestant prayer meetings at the home of Flo Dodge where they "got a real taste of Christian unity in the power of the Holy Spirit . . . This meeting of men and women from such radically different backgrounds could only have taken place with the grace of God."[7]

The ecumenical ideal shared by Patti and many other early Charismatics was certainly present in the early stages of the CCR as a whole. However, the Catholic movement soon began to diverge from the Protestant renewal in significant ways. Where the Protestants tended to separate from the mainline churches and to form various Pentecostal sects, the Catholic Charismatics held tightly to their identification as a movement within the established Roman Catholic Church. To this effect, Catholic Charismatics formed prayer groups and Charismatic communities which met regularly within the parish framework whenever possible, but also in independent renewal centers and covenant communities, which began to emerge in large numbers.

The early years of the CCR movement were largely concerned with defining and establishing the relationship between individual experience of the Spirit and the sacraments and traditions of the church. One of the first questions that needed to be addressed by the CCR was the relationship between the sacraments of initiation and the "baptism in the Spirit" which most of the converts had undergone. In 1973, Cardinal Leon Josef Suenens, appointed by Pope Paul VI as special advisor in overseeing the reception of the CCR into the life of the church, issued a series of documents, known as the "Malines documents," in which he addressed various issues on the Renewal movement. The first Malines document distinguished between the actual conferral of the Spirit in the sacraments and coming to an experiential awareness of the gift already received.[8] It came to be understood within the movement that the Spirit, which had been bestowed on each Catholic at baptism, was experienced anew in the spiritual rebirth known as "baptism in the Spirit."

The 1980s saw a continued emphasis within the movement on strengthening the CCR's position as a legitimate and accepted movement within the church. In spite of the church's official recognition and a number of papal statements confirming acceptance of the movement, many Charismatics still felt relegated to the fringes of church life. However, the conviction persisted that the Spirit was working through the movement in order to effect renewal throughout the entire church, and so Charismatics remained focused on bringing the energy of renewal into ecclesiastical life, not only personally but structurally as well.

The CCR began to take on new structures, both in local dioceses and internationally. In 1981, the worldwide headquarters of the CCR was moved from Brussels to Rome, where it was renamed the International Catholic Charismatic Renewal Office (ICCRO). This change, of course, brought the Renewal movement closer to the administrative and spiritual center of the church, but it also represented a "lessening in the ecumenical thrust of CCR."[9] It also was indicative of a centralizing trend in the movement away from the local prayer groups and covenant communities, which had, during the late 1980s, undergone a series of major crises over matters of leadership and authority. Patti Mansfield was concerned about the state of affairs within the movement. In July of 1987, she wrote, "I was distressed over the state of the Charismatic Renewal in the United States, which, in my opinion, was in great need of purification, of inner unity and of empowerment."[10]

One community that experienced a particularly serious crisis was the Word of God community in Ann Arbor, Michigan, led by Ralph Martin and Steve Clark. Tensions between the two leaders resulted in a 1990 split, with Ralph Martin continuing in the leadership role of the Word of God community, and Steve Clark and Bruce Yokum forming a new community called the Washtenaw Covenant Community.[11]

As a result of this separation and other tensions among the covenant community leadership, the CCR's National Service Committee, whose membership had previously been comprised of leaders of major communities, shifted to a membership of diocesan leaders, resulting in a network of Diocesan Service Committees, thereby replacing the single National Service Committee. By the late 1980s there were about eighty Diocesan Renewal Centers serving the CCR.[12] By the 1990s, the movement had become significantly more centralized, with institutions such as the Franciscan University of Steubenville, headed by Fr. Michael Scanlan, a Charismatic Franciscan priest, assuming special importance.[13]

Thus, the 1980s and 1990s saw the CCR move into a more clearly defined "Catholic" movement firmly established within the church and with less of an ecumenical focus. The period also witnessed the strengthening of a spirit of evangelization, within the church to be sure, but also especially within the CCR. The evangelization effort came to be focused more on bringing the Spirit into the rest of the world and particularly into the "Third World."

DEMOGRAPHIC CHANGES

The CCR, as stated previously, has not only survived, but, at the beginning of the 21st Century, it thrives in over 235 countries worldwide. However, significant changes have occurred in the movement's demographic makeup during the forty years of its existence.

The 1970s and early 1980s were a period of self-identification and rapid growth for the Renewal movement. In a very short period of time, the movement attracted large numbers of converts, primarily among white, middle class college students. Patti Mansfield writes that the first conference of Catholic Charismatics that she attended took place at Notre Dame University in September, 1967, where fifty people had gathered. By 1973, the Catholic Charismatic Conference that again met at Notre Dame was held in a football stadium, with 35,000 Charismatics in attendance.[14] By the turn of the century, the World Christian Encyclopedia reported a figure of 9,742,000 Catholic Charismatics in North America alone.[15] Clearly, the movement had enjoyed a steady increase in the number of members through the end of the 20th Century.

During the 1980s, however, as tensions within the movement were leading to fractured local leadership and a resulting centralizing trend, another shift was taking place. While the CCR had from its earliest days a concern with spreading the word about baptism in the Spirit, as the movement moved into the 1970s and 1980s there emerged an even stronger emphasis on evangelization. As early as 1975 Pope Paul VI's letter *Evangelii Nuntiandi* had stimulated enthusiasm among Charismatics. They responded energetically, forming evangelization fellowships in places like Mexico City (Fellowship of Communities of Evangelization in the Holy Spirit) and Malta (Glory of God Covenant Community and the International Catholic Programme of Evangelization).[16] Evangelization, which had always been characteristic of the Protestant Pentecostal churches, began to take on a much greater significance in the Catholic renewal movement as the words of Acts 4:20[17] became a reality among CCR participants. These words of St. Paul, which referred to the evangelizing mission of the original apostles, have become a motto of the modern-day evangelizing mission of the CCR.[18]

During the 1980s, the evangelizing focus shifted from North America to what was then known as the "Third World." As growth began to slow in the United States, it increased dramatically in Africa, Asia, and Latin America.[19] Reflecting upon the missionary zeal of the CCR, Archbishop Paul Josef Cordes, President of the Pontifical Council *Cor Unum*, wrote, "One of the evident fruits of 'Baptism in the Spirit' is the desire to evangelize, to announce the Good News of salvation to the whole world."[20]

Papal support for the evangelizing mission has also been evident. On the mission of the church and the faithful to evangelize, Pope Paul VI wrote: "For the Church, evangelization means bringing the Good News into all strata of humanity, and through its influence transforming humanity from within and making it new."[21] Pope John Paul II, in his post-synodal[22] Apostolic Exhortation *Christifideles Laici,* exhorted Catholics to a renewed evangelical mission: "The vocation to holiness is intimately connected to mission and to the responsibility entrusted to the lay faithful in the Church and in the world."[23]

The desire to spread the good news that the Spirit was available and willing to bestow grace and charisms upon church members took on a new urgency as CCR participants undertook the mission of worldwide evangelization. By the year 2000, over 11 percent of Catholics worldwide identified themselves as Charismatics, with a reported 8,771,000 Catholic Charismatics in Africa (7%), 16,422,000 in Asia (15%), 73,604,000 in Latin America (16%), some 350,000 in Oceania (4%), and even 100 in Antarctica (7%).[24] Efforts to evangelize Africa, Asia, and Latin America were particularly successful. In "A Preferential Option for the Spirit: the Catholic Charismatic Renewal in Latin America's New Religious Economy," Andrew R. Chestnut writes:

> Latin American Charismatics probably number between 22 million and 25 million, accounting for approximately one-third of the global total (Comunicado Mensal 1997). With a Charismatic community of between 8 and 10 million, Brazil constitutes the center of gravity of the Latin American CCR. Since less than 10 percent of Brazil's 122 million self-proclaimed Catholics actively participate in church life, it is very likely that at least half of all active Catholics in Brazil are Charismatics. Data for other Latin American countries are lacking, but the CCR is the largest and most active Catholic lay movement in most nations.[25]

Why was the CCR so particularly successful in Latin America? Since the 1950s, Protestant Pentecostalism had been on the rise in Latin America, and by the 1980s and 1990s the flow of Catholics into Pentecostal churches had increased dramatically. Chestnut explains that the Latin American bishops saw the CCR as a viable and legitimate means of staunching the flow of Latin American Catholics into the Pentecostal churches, and, therefore, despite fears that the CCR might represent a threat to episcopal authority, most bishops welcomed the movement and supported CCR-sponsored programs.[26]

Among the first Latin American Bishops to embrace the CCR were Carlos Talavera of Mexico and Diego Jaramillo of Colombia. On the other hand, there was also significant opposition. The conservative Bishop Miguel Garcia of Mazatlan, Mexico banned the Renewal from his diocese, calling it the "smoke of Satan that has infiltrated the Church."[27] Bishop Antonio Lopez of Durango,

Mexico, who also proscribed the CCR in his diocese, accused the movement of "elitism, fundamentalism, Protestant contamination, charismania [excessive emphasis on spiritual gifts], paraclericalism, and authoritarianism."[28]

Nevertheless, the CCR continued to expand in Latin America, as well as in Asia and in Africa, areas that had also already experienced the rapid growth of Protestant Pentecostalism. Philip Jenkins theorizes that one possible reason for the attraction to Pentecostal movements in Third World countries may have been the desire of the poor for the healing experience offered by Pentecostalism. In fact, he considers healing the "key element that has allowed Christianity to compete so successfully with its rivals outside the Christian tradition, with traditional religion in Africa, with various animist and spiritist movements of African origin in Brazil, with shamanism in Korea . . . Issues of healing, whether of mind or body, dominate the everyday life of the churches of the poor."[29] Jenkins also quotes Andrew Chestnut, who argues that "More than any other reason, it is the desire to be cured of alcoholism that impels Brazilian men to convert to Pentecostalism."[30] In sub-Saharan Africa, where over two-thirds of all AIDS cases worldwide are found, Pentecostalism and the CCR thrive. Harvey Cox also points out that, "there can be little doubt that what one finds in the Yoido Full Gospel Church of Seoul involves a massive importation of shamanic [healing] practice into a Christian ritual."[31] A desire for healing on the part of the poor, who are unable to benefit from the advances of modern science and medicine, is readily apparent in developing countries, and the promise of faith healing offered by Pentecostal or Charismatic communities easily becomes an attractive alternative. In addition, it would appear that the sense of empowerment that Pentecostalism offers to the poor and the marginalized is a strong attraction for people of the post-colonial developing world.

Whether for reasons of healing, empowerment of the disenfranchised, or genuine religious conversion (or a combination of these), the CCR has enjoyed remarkable success in its efforts to evangelize the developing nations of the world. It is in this area that the most striking changes in the movement late in the 20th century may be discerned, along with the shift from small local covenant communities to a more centralized structural organization.

Still, while the ecumenical roots of the movement seemed in some ways to be eclipsed by the thrust toward evangelization, certain key voices continued the earlier emphasis on ecumenical unity. Archbishop Paul Josef Cordes, for example, wrote that, "The tension between the experienced need to give common witness to the Gospel message and the limitations set by the differences arising from the continuing disunity among Christians is a call to prayer and to a search for an ever broader commonality in truth. The Charismatic Renewal offers much common ground for this process."[32] The Renewal, then, sought not only to evangelize the world, but also to bring together all Christians in a common experience of the Spirit.

The "common experience of the Spirit" is an important aspect of the CCR, which looks back to the events of the first Pentecost after the death of Jesus as a model for Charismatic life in the present. Just as the apostles, who were gathered together in a communal assembly, all received the gifts of the Spirit as it descended on them simultaneously, Charismatics also seek a shared encounter with the Spirit. The charisms of the Spirit, glossolalia, prophecy, and healing, are gifts to be shared with each other in a common experience that is essential to Charismatic spirituality.

NOTES

1. Mansfield, *As By a New Pentecost,* 35.
2. World Christian Encyclopedia, (accessed 15 May 2008); available from: http://www.iccrs.org/CCR%20worldwide.htm; Internet.
3. The Pew Forum on Religion and Public Life. *Spirit and Power: A 10-Country Survey of Pentecostals*; (accessed 31 May 08); available from: http://pewforum.org/newassets/surveys/pentecostal/pentecostals-08.pdf, p. 93; Internet.
4. Peter Hocken, "The Catholic Charismatic Renewal." In Vinson Synan, *The Century of the Holy Spirit: 100 Years of Pentecostal and Charismatic Renewal* (Nashville: Thomas Nelson Publishers, 2001), 211.
5. Ibid.
6. Mansfield, *As By a New Pentecost,* 54-55, 61.
7. Ibid., 27.
8. Hocken, *The Catholic Charismatic Renewal*, 216-217.
9. Ibid., 220.
10. Mansfield, *As By a New Pentecost,* 167.
11. Hocken, The *Catholic Charismatic Renewal*, 221.
12. Ibid.
13. Ibid., 223.
14. Mansfield, *As By a New Pentecost,* 65.
15. World Christian Encyclopedia, (accessed 31 May 2008); available from: http://www.iccrs.org/CCR%20worldwide.htm; Internet.
16. Hocken, *The Catholic Charismatic Renewal*, 224.
17. "We cannot help but speak of what we have seen and heard."
18. Mansfield, *As By a New Pentecost,* 31.
19. Hocken, The *Catholic Charismatic Renewal*, 225.
20. Cordes, *Call to Holiness,* 38.
21. Pope Paul VI, *Evangelii nuntiandi,* 18.
22. The 1987 Synod of Bishops included over two hundred bishops from 92 countries as well as a number of lay observers, and topics addressed included the status

of women in the church, the role of the laity, and the responsibilities of Catholic politicians.

23. Pope John Paul II, *Christifideles laici,* 17.

24. World Christian Encyclopedia, (accessed 31 May 2008); available from: http://www.iccrs.org/CCR%20worldwide.htm; Internet.

25. Andrew R. Chesnut, "A Preferential Option for the Spirit: the Catholic Charismatic Renewal in Latin America's New Religious Economy," *Latin American Politics and Society.* Spring, 2003; (accessed 6 June 2008); available from: http://findarticles.com/p/articles/mi_qa4000/is_200304/ai_n9210859/pg_6; Internet.

26. Ibid.

27. Chesnut, Andrew R., *Competitive Spirits: Latin America's New Religious Economy* (New York: Oxford University Press, 2003), 72

28. Andrew R. Chesnut, "A Preferential Option for the Spirit: the Catholic Charismatic Renewal in Latin America's New Religious Economy," *Latin American Politics and Society.* Spring, 2003; (accessed 6 June 2008); available from: http://findarticles.com/p/articles/mi_qa4000/is_200304/ai_n9210859/pg_6; Internet.

29. Philip Jenkins, *The Next Christendom: The Coming of Global Christianity* (New York: Oxford University Press, 2002), 126.

30. Quoted in Jenkins, *The Next Christendom,* 126.

31. Ibid.

32. Cordes, *Call to Holiness,* 68.

Chapter Six

Charismatic Spirituality

What exactly is "spirituality"? Merriam-Webster defines "spirit," derived from the Latin *spirare*, "to breathe," as "an animating or vital principle held to give life to physical organisms." The word "spirit," then, connotes the connection between breath and life, and so "spirit" may be considered to be the "life-giving force" of human existence. This connection is not new; the Hebrew *ruach* and the Greek *pneuma*, as well as the Sanskrit *prana*, all share the double meanings of "breath" and "spirit." The Hebrew *ruach* can also mean "wind." Thus, the Hebrew scriptures contain the metaphor of the wind (*ruach*) as the breath or the spirit of God.

The English word "inspiration," literally means, of course, to "breathe in." But the word as defined by Merriam-Webster also refers to "a divine influence or action on a person believed to qualify him or her to receive and communicate sacred revelation." The connection among breath, life, spirit, and God is ancient and deeply rooted in human thought and experience. Spirituality, then, may be thought of as that force or power that enlivens and radically connects human existence with the divine.

Christianity inherits its concept of Spirit from the Hebrew *ruach*. *Ruach*, translated into the Greek *pneuma*, is the term used by Jesus in the gospels to refer to the Spirit. The book of Acts tells us that on the day of Pentecost, the Apostles were gathered all in one place, when "suddenly a sound came from heaven like the rush of a mighty wind (*pnoe*), and it filled all the house where they were sitting. And there appeared to them tongues as of fire, distributed and resting on each one of them. And they were all filled with the Holy Spirit (*pneuma*) and began to speak in other tongues, as the Spirit (*pneuma*) gave them utterance" (Acts 2: 1-4 Oxford RSV).

Historically, Christian spirituality was delineated in the early years by Paul of Tarsus in his letters to the communities he established in his travels. Pauline spirituality focuses on the death and resurrection of Jesus (Romans 3-8; 1 Corinthians 15), on life in the Spirit (Romans 8), on the gifts (charisms) of the Spirit (1 Corinthians 12-14), on faith, hope, and love as the qualities of a true Christian (1 Corinthians 13). He describes "spiritual life" as a life of freedom, specifically freedom from the law (Galatians 3-5).[1]

Over the next six centuries, other themes also developed in Christian spirituality: worship and sacraments, witness unto death, spiritual disciplines, monasticism, and mysticism. But the early Christian focus on charisms persisted, even as their importance was debated among the church fathers.[2]

During the Middle Ages, Eastern Orthodox Christianity preserved a monastic, meditative, inner focus on spiritual experience, whereas the Roman Catholic church developed and nurtured an appreciation for intellectual understanding and visible signs of God's work in the world. The Orthodox, for their part, primarily emphasized an *apophatic* and *hesychastic* spirituality, whereas the scholastic tradition in the West developed a more *kataphatic* approach.[3] Catholic Charismatics, like Protestant Pentecostals, look back to the earliest days of Christianity and identify with the experience of the apostles following the first Pentecost after Jesus' death and resurrection. Charismatics and Pentecostals both continue to put high value on a personal relationship with the Spirit and the gifts that the Spirit bestows.

However, whereas Protestant Pentecostals have broken away from the mainline Protestant churches, Catholic Charismatics strive for a particularly close and personal relationship with the triune God as professed by the Catholic church, and identify themselves unequivocally as members of that church. They see themselves not as a group chosen by the Spirit to break off from the church, but rather as a group called to renew the church and facilitate the realignment of the church with the work of the Spirit. Thus, Catholic Charismatics honor the Pope and conform to Catholic traditions and policies. It is not uncommon, for example, for Catholic Charismatics to pray to Jesus, or Mary, or simply to "God." However, there exists a particularly strong emphasis on the Spirit, and the gifts that the Spirit bestows.

Charismatic spirituality emerges from a desire for a personal transcendent experience, or an experience of the "Spirit," as well as a continuing personal relationship with the Spirit. The "Spirit" is perceived to be the actual spirit (life or breath) of God, which is believed to function through the gifts, or charisms, that it confers on those who open themselves to invitation, such as happened during the Duquesne Weekend. At that weekend, and at subsequent Charismatic gatherings, the hymn *Veni Creator Spiritus* (Come Creator Spirit) was sung as an invocation and an invitation to the Holy Spirit to fill the hearts of the faithful, and participants formulated a conscious intention "to keep on praying this until the Holy Spirit comes."[4] At the 40th Anniversary Catholic

Charismatic Conference in Steubenville, Ohio, in June, 2007,[5] this prayer was sung in English (*Come Holy Ghost*) at the opening session as well as at other sessions during the weekend of the conference. The participants stood, arms raised, palms facing outward, and sang the hymn as an invocation to the Spirit and a conscious invitation to fill the hearts of those present.[6] When questioned, a participant told me that this posture represents "an attitude of surrender that opens the heart and invites the Spirit to dwell there."

The attitude of surrender seems to be an essential prerequisite to the Charismatic experience. Patti Gallagher Mansfield, in her description of her baptism in the Spirit, writes that the experience began for her immediately after she prayed what she calls "a prayer of unconditional surrender," where she offered her life to God: "I give my life to You, and whatever You want of me, that's what I choose. If it means suffering, then I accept that."[7]

Marybeth Mutmansky, another Duquesne weekend participant, also writes that she offered a prayer of surrender the night before the retreat began: "I don't want to fight You. From now on, whatever You want in my life, I want, too."[8] These sentiments are echoed by other participants in the Duquesne retreat. Paul Gray and Maryann Springel, writing about their Duquesne experience, testified: "We gave our lives to Jesus, and he gave us His Holy Spirit."[9] Receiving the gifts of the Holy Spirit is known among Charismatics as "Baptism in the Spirit." Those who are baptized in the Spirit typically display the *charisms*, or gifts, that the Spirit bestows. These include speaking in tongues (glossolalia), prophecy, and healing.

GLOSSOLALIA

The practice of speaking in tongues does not originate with Christianity, nor is its expression limited to Christianity. The ancient Egyptians wrote about cases of "ecstatic utterances of a divinely inspired nature," and the prophecies of the oracles of Delphi, Dodona, and Epirus appear to be related to glossolalia.[10] Christians refer to a passage in the Acts of the Apostles that describes the descent of the Holy Spirit upon the apostles on the day of Pentecost:

And there appeared to them tongues as of fire, distributed and resting on each one of them. And they were all filled with the Holy Spirit and began to speak in other tongues, as the Spirit gave them utterance. (Acts 2: 3, 4; RSV)

This event is commonly understood to mean that the apostles were given the gift of speaking in human languages such that each foreign listener could understand them in his own language. However, according to at least one psychological study of the phenomenon, "today there are no verifiable instances of a tongue-speaker having a foreign language at his command which he has not learned by the usual means."[11] Nevertheless, Patti Gallagher Mansfield writes of at least one instance where she claims to have heard someone pray in a foreign language:

> One night at a prayer meeting I sat next to David Mangan who had already received the gift of tongues. I was flabbergasted as I heard David pray in beautiful, flowing French. It sounded like the words of a psalm, praising the kindness of the Divine Child, extolling the streams of living water. The cadence of his French was different, but his pronunciation was perfect. After the meeting I asked David if he knew he had been praying in French; he didn't. I was impressed by the authenticity of this charismatic gift. It was a sign to me that God was at work.[12]

Glossolalia as it is practiced in modern times manifests itself in such a way that the speaker utters syllables, words, and phrases that they have never heard before and do not understand. The person may speak just a few syllables, or they may go on for several minutes. Glossolalia, in spite of Patti Gallagher Mansfield's report cited above, is not usually understood to mean that a person is speaking a foreign earthly language unknown to the speaker, but rather that the speaker is receiving a message from God and speaking in a "heavenly" language not normally understood by humans. Others, who claim to have received the gift of interpretation, may hear these heavenly words or syllables and translate the message for others.

Today, it is expected among Charismatics that every new convert will experience the gift of speaking in tongues, which is seen as evidence that one has received baptism in the Spirit. However, the early church Fathers were ambiguous about this particular gift, which was not always distinguished from the gift of prophecy. Irenaeus, for example, substitutes the word "prophesy" for "speaking in tongues" in writing about the apostle Peter's visit to Caesarea.[13] Glossolalia was also famously practiced by Montanus, a heretical Christian from Phrygia who prophesied the imminent end of the world. Origen, John Chrysostom, and Augustine of Hippo all considered the use of glossolalia a gift that was relevant to biblical times, but which had since passed away.[14]

Still, the practice has persisted with varying degrees of acceptance. The Ranters of England, a splinter group of Quakers, claimed to experience glossolalia. Edward Irving, a Presbyterian pastor in London, encouraged the practice and founded a new sect he called the Catholic Apostolic Church, which lasted for about forty years after his death in 1834.[15] The Pentecostal Church, which emerged in the United States in the early 20th Century, views glossolalia as an integral part of the Pentecostal experience, and the Catholic Charismatics certainly embrace the practice as evidence of true conversion.

PROPHECY

Prophecy, defined by the Pew Forum as "A spontaneous utterance spoken in worship settings believed to be inspired by the Holy Spirit," is another of the charisms observed among Catholic Charismatics. It is not necessarily understood as a prediction of future events; rather, it generally is seen as a divine "message" conveyed through the participant. Prophecy is generally communicated in the native language of the speaker.

During the course of the Duquesne Weekend, Patti Gallagher Mansfield recorded "words that kept coming to mind throughout the day" and which she and others later "realized . . . was the charismatic gift of prophecy." Examples of these "messages from the Lord" recorded by Mansfield include:

> My love exceeds all you can imagine, My love for you. How much I give to all who ask. Do not be too proud to come for help. I am with you always – just waiting for your surrender, your "yes" . . . Live a new life of trust . . . You will know Me. And in Me, My Father. And in Me, My Spirit.

Also,

> Listen, my children, to the sound of My voice. You know Me – I live in the depths of your being . . . If only you would trust Me, you would see how simple life is moment by moment.[16]

According to the Pew Forum on Religion and Public Life, 39% of Charismatics in the United States claim to have had a "direct revelation from God." In the 2006 study, 63% of Charismatics in Guatemala, 78% in Kenya, 61% in India, and 61% in South Korea made similar claims. In most cases, the percentage of Protestant Pentecostals was even higher.[17] As prophecy is considered to flow out of a direct connection with God, who is assumed to speak through the prophet, it is significant that so many Charismatics and Pentecostals claim to have had revelatory or prophetic experiences.

HEALING

Faith healing has been an integral part of religious experience since the earliest days of human history. Neolithic paintings show representations of shaman-like figures. Archeological evidence of shamanic practice has been discovered on six continents.[18] Witch doctors, medicine men, and shamans[19] have all been seen as channels of supernatural healing energy, and people have looked to them for physical cures, mental and emotional comfort, and spiritual peace. In spite of Enlightenment thought and the advances of modern science, belief in the healing powers of prayer and religious experience has persisted to modern times, where it is evidenced in phenomena such as New Age spirituality, alternative healing methods, and in Pentecostal and Charismatic spiritual movements.

In the Catholic Charismatic movement, healing as a gift of the Spirit appears shortly after the Duquesne Weekend. Patti Gallagher Mansfield writes that after she returned to school following the events of the Duquesne Weekend retreat, she came to know that her dormitory housemother, Mrs. Jones, was in the hospital with phlebitis. Mansfield writes: "As I read the note, a thought went through my mind: 'Go, lay your hands on her, and she will be healed.'" The next day, her hands tingling, she went to see Mrs. Jones in the hospital, where she traced a cross on the forehead of the patient saying, "I know you're going to be all right, Mrs. Jones." Some days later, Mansfield was surprised to see Mrs. Jones in the school cafeteria, where Mrs. Jones explained that "the swelling had gone down more quickly than expected, and the doctors had discharged her." Mansfield writes that she believed that her prayer "helped speed the healing process."[20]

The charism of healing is not understood solely to apply to physical healing. The "true" healing associated with the CCR is a healing of the soul, a reordering of one's life and mind that brings it into alignment with the will of God. In discussing the charism of healing, Archbishop Paul Josef Cordes, appointed by Pope John Paul II as Episcopal Advisor to the International Catholic Charismatic Renewal Office in Rome, and later President of the Pontifical Council *Cor Unum*,[21] has written that, "this healing addresses the full complement of human suffering: the spiritual, the emotional, the psychological, and the social – as well as the physical . . . it is a part of the encounter with the living Lord and of conversion of the heart."[22]

Charismatic spirituality is essentially based on a personal encounter with the "living Lord" to which Archbishop Cordes refers. The charisms that appear as manifestations of this personal encounter are considered both a part of the process of and as evidence of the conversion of the heart. Charismatics invoke the Spirit in order to achieve, and then to maintain, a personal and lasting conversion that will result in the relief of the "full complement" of human suffering and facilitate the work of the Spirit in the world.

CATHOLIC CHARISMATIC SPIRITUALITIES

Charismatic spirituality is characterized by an emphasis on the experience of charisms, or gifts of the Spirit. Glossolalia, prophecy, and spiritual and physical healing are considered to be signs that the Holy Spirit is active in and through the life of the practitioner. A Charismatic aspirant prays for and expects these gifts, and rejoices to experience any or all of them.

The Catholic tradition has a long and varied history of spirituality and spiritual expression. Certainly, the gospel tradition makes it clear that the apostles experienced the gifts of the Spirit on the occasion of the first Pentecost after the departure of Jesus, and that other Christians of the time also sought and received those gifts. However, ambivalence about charismatic gifts has also existed from Christianity's inception. In his first letter to the Corinthians, St. Paul, while exhorting his readers to "eagerly desire" spiritual gifts, nevertheless, cautions that the gift of prophecy is preferable to the gift of tongues, which he saw as too mysterious and unintelligible for the average person unless the tongue-speaker also received the gift of prophecy and the ability to interpret the heavenly language. Eminently practical, Paul says, "I thank God that I speak in tongues more than all of you. Nevertheless, in church I would rather speak five words with my mind in order to instruct others, than ten thousand words in a tongue."[23] Church fathers such as Irenaeus, Origen, John Chrysostom, and Augustine of Hippo wrote cautiously if not disparagingly about the gift of tongues and its uses. Augustine wrote that glossolalia was a phenomenon that, while it may have been useful during the apostolic period, had nevertheless passed away by his own time. He, too, seems to have agreed with Paul that prophecy was a more dependable, and, therefore preferable charism.[24]

Augustine, who "championed the grace of God against human effort as the means of salvation," harbored suspicion about spirituality that seemed to depend overmuch on the efforts of the seeker, and he insisted that spirituality and its gifts come only through the grace of God.[25] This view influenced subsequent church attitudes toward spirituality, so that to actively seek the gifts of the Spirit was not encouraged until the Reformation era. As a result, charismatic spirituality, which receives a degree of emphasis in the early Christian writings, declined as a result of the influence of the theology of grace espoused by Augustine and his successors in the Western mainstream church.

On the other hand, in the East, the 6th-century Neoplatonist theology of Dionysius, an anonymous Syrian monk (also sometimes referred to as "pseudo-Dionysius" or "Dionysius the Areopagite") who was "perhaps the single greatest influence on the development of Christian mysticism,"[26] encouraged ecstatic mystical spirituality. His articulation of three stages of spiritual development included and emphasized a unitive experience of oneness with God. Dionysius stressed an apophatic approach that asserted that God was beyond any and all attributes and could only be known after entering "a darkness that is beyond understanding."[27]

There is little evidence that charismatic gifts were widespread in Christian spirituality during the medieval period. It was not until the years following the Protestant Reformation that charismatic gifts once again became popular expressions of spirituality, and then primarily among non-Catholic sects such as the Anabaptists, Huguenots, the Jansenists, and the Ranters (an English radical dissenter group famous for their ecstatic shouting during their worship services). During the 19th century, there are documented cases of glossolalia experiences in Scandinavia and orthodox Russia. In the United States, the Church of Latter Day Saints included in its articles of faith an emphasis on "the gifts of tongues, prophecy, revelation, visions, healing, interpretation of tongues, etc."[28]

While Catholic spirituality has not historically emphasized the charismatic gifts, a strong mystical tradition has persisted in spite of the Church's view that "the vision of God is the work of grace and the reward of eternal life; in the present life only a few souls, by a special grace, can reach it."[29] Since the Middle Ages the Catholic church has emphasized the Scholastic predilection for reason over emotion, and before the 14th century invention in Europe of the printing press, stood as the sole reader and interpreter of scripture for all the faithful. Nevertheless, 15th century mystics such as Teresa of Avila, John of the Cross, and the 12th century abbess Hildegard von Bingen are stellar examples of aspirants who not only achieved the mystical state, but recorded their experiences so that others could follow in their footsteps.

The Protestant churches, on the other hand, embrace Martin Luther's principles of personal, unmediated relationship with God, as well as the responsibility of each individual to read and interpret scripture for themselves. Thus, the gifts bestowed on the apostles and early Christians have not only been well known to scripture-reading Protestants, but they have also been desired and encouraged by Protestants who consider themselves to be part of the "priesthood of all believers." It is no surprise, then, that in 1906, when the Pentecostal movement emerged on Azusa Street in Los Angeles, charisms such as glossolalia came to be seen as evidence of the favor of the Spirit and that the gifts of the Spirit would become characteristic of the Pentecostal churches. The early Catholic Charismatics were certainly familiar with Pentecostal spirituality, and Peter Collins, who discovered the book *They Speak with Other Tongues* while visiting a Pentecostal church, later gave a copy of the book to Steve Clark, a Cursillo member who would become a founding member of the Catholic Charismatic Renewal movement.[30]

Charismatic spirituality, then, has ancient origins and has been present in Christian experience since the early days of the faith. However, it has also been viewed by mainline theology with suspicion as something dangerous and capable of deviation. The CCR identified with the spiritual tradition of the early church and, in effect, also revived the Medieval mystical tradition of Western Catholicism during the second half of the 20th Century.

NOTES

1. Bradley P. Holt, *Thirsty for God: A Brief History of Christian Spirituality*.(M inneapolis: Fortress Press, 2005), 38.

2. Kildahl, *Psychology of Speaking in Tongues*, 14-15.

3. *Apophatic* spirituality refers to the understanding of God as described by what God is *not* (*via negativa*), or in terms of a God without or beyond attributes. *Kataphatic* spirituality defines God in terms of what God *is,* or as having positive attributes. *Apophatic* spirituality represents a more internal, non-verbal approach to encountering God within the human heart, while *kataphatic* spirituality is aligned with an intellectual path to the divine.

4. Mansfield, *As By a New Pentecost*, 35.

5. See note #137.

6. Standing or kneeling with upraised arms and open, outward-facing palms, is typical of the Charismatic prayer posture.

7. Mansfield, *As By a New Pentecost*, 39.

8. Ibid., 67.

9. Ibid., 72.

10. Kidahl, *Psychology of Speaking in Tongues*, 11. I personally observed this kind of behavior among participants in yogic meditation retreats where it is seen as a movement of *Shakti* (a Sanskrit word describing conscious, awakened, spiritual energy).

11. Ibid., 13.

12. Mansfield, *As By a New Pentecost*, 50.

13. Acts: 10.

14. Kildahl, *Psychology of Speaking in Tongues*, 14.

15. Ibid., 17.

16. Mansfield, *As By a New Pentecost*, 49.

17. The Pew Forum on Religion and Public Life. *Spirit and Power: A 10-Country Survey of Pentecostals*; (accessed 31 May 08); available from: http://pewforum.org/newassets/surveys/pentecostal/pentecostals-08.pdf, p. 93; Internet.

18. Jay H. Bernstein, *Spirits Captured in Stone: Shamanism and Traditional Medicine among the Taman of Borneo* (Boulder: Lynne Rienner Publishers, 1997), 3.

19. A "medicine man" (indigenous North American cultures), "witch doctor" (African cultures), or "shaman" (Siberian and Central Asian cultures) is one who is thought to act as an intermediary between the material and the spirit worlds.

20. Mansfield, *As By a New Pentecost*, 52.

21. The Pontifical Council *Cor Unum* ("one heart") was established by Pope Paul VI in July 1971 for the purpose of aiding the poor and fostering integral human development.

22. Cordes, *Call to Holiness,* 53.
23. 1Corinthians 14: 18-19.
24. Cited by Kildahl, *Psychology of Speaking in Tongues,* 14-15.
25. Holt, *Thirsty for God,* 72.
26. Philip Sheldrake, *A Brief History of Spirituality* (Malden: Blackwell, 2007), 31.
27. Holt, *Thirst for God,* 73. In addition to the ultimate unitive stage of spiritual development, Dionysius included a purgative and an illuminative stage. See also Alister E. McGrath, *Christian Spirituality* (Malden: Blackwell, 1999), 118.
28. Ibid., 17-18.
29. New Advent Catholic Encyclopedia; (accessed 19 July 2008); available from: http://home.newadvent.org/cathen/10663b.htm; Internet.
30. Mansfield, *As By a New Pentecost,* 12.

Chapter Seven

Conclusion

As has been described in Chapter I, the 1960s were a decade of pivotal change in the United States and in the world. The post-World War II generation saw the civil rights movement, the feminist movement, and the anti-Vietnam war movements emerge as responses to the desire for a holistic society where all people would be free and would be able to live in a culture based on ideals of peace, harmony, and freedom. In addition to the political and social movements, however, many people looked to religion for renewal and new meaning. Eastern religions became popular in the United States, but many Americans also looked to their own religious roots for guidance. The Protestant Pentecostal movement, which had been in existence since the beginning of the century, began to expand dramatically, and other religious groups began to experience renewal as well.

Patti Mansfield and other Catholics who felt a similar yearning for spiritual renewal saw the object of their longing as the "Spirit" of God, and they perceived their experiences of speaking in tongues, prophecy, and healing as the work of the Holy Spirit made manifest through them. As committed Catholics, they looked for, and found, validation in the writings and documents of the church and the popes, and they were convinced of their calling to act as channels of spiritual energy such that the church might once again be enlivened and aligned with the work of the Spirit. Some influential members of the church hierarchy, like Cardinal Suenens, recognized the movement as a legitimate expression of the Holy Spirit, and sought to legitimize the group and its aims. The early years of the CCR saw rapid growth as the movement sought to define and to establish itself within the church.

In reviewing the history of the CCR, several historical trends have become apparent:

1) While both the CCR and the Protestant Pentecostal movements showed a strong trend toward ecumenism, the CCR seems to have lost some of its original ecumenical enthusiasm in exchange for church acceptance;
2) With church acceptance and its own rapid growth, the CCR also necessarily lost some of its original spontaneity as it structured itself to meet the exigencies of growing membership and to conform to church guidelines;
3) Toward the end of the 20th century, the CCR began a dramatic worldwide expansion, and it became especially popular among Catholics in the developing world. This development has resulted in a shift in the United States from a mostly white, middle-class Charismatic membership to a growing number of Catholic Charismatic Latino immigrants. This trend appears to be continuing.
4) Much like the Protestant Pentecostals, the Catholic Charismatic movement has both demonstrated a resiliency and an ability to adapt that has enabled it not only to survive the changes of the 20th century, but to expand and to thrive, demonstrating continued vitality and appeal both at home and abroad.

ECUMENISM

As seen in Chapter IV, both the Protestant Pentecostal movement and the CCR demonstrated a strong interest in ecumenism.[1] Many of the early Catholic Charismatics, including some of the participants in the Duquesne weekend, participated in Protestant prayer groups where they first observed what they identified as manifestations of the Spirit, i.e., glossolalia, prophecy, and faith healing.[2] Patti Gallagher Mansfield expresses special gratitude to Flo Dodge, the leader of a Protestant prayer group that Mansfield attended, for providing insight into Pentecostal spirituality "which gave birth to such a powerful move of the Holy Spirit among Catholics."[3] However, as the CCR gained acceptance into the church, its focus came to be redirected toward a stronger Catholic identity in order to avoid any accusations of being a splinter group or of causing divisiveness within the church. So there seems to have been a sacrifice of ecumenism in exchange for church acceptance.

LOSS OF SPONTANEITY AND WORLDWIDE EXPANSION

Throughout the late 1960s and the 1970s, the CCR spread primarily and most rapidly among college campuses in the United States. Groups of people on college retreats seemed spontaneously to be baptized in the Spirit, and as word spread from one college to another, more and more people were attracted to the movement. People like Patti Mansfield, Ralph Martin, and Steve Clark were instrumental in expanding the movement and in bringing the principles and practices of the Cursillo program to the nascent CCR. The CCR arose during the 1960s as a spontaneous expression of the need felt by some Catholics for a closer, more personal relationship with God through direct experience of the Spirit. Yet this search for spiritual meaning and faith renewal remained within the context of their church community. During the 1980s and 1990s the CCR gained large numbers of followers as well as ecclesial acceptance, and it took on an organizational structure that would allow it to fit within the larger church establishment. As it began to conform to the demands of bureaucracy, however, it began to lose some of its original spontaneity. This process led to some speculation that the movement was beginning to wane. But this was not the case. During the 1990s, the CCR, like the Pentecostal movement before it, began to gain wide acceptance outside the United States, and especially in the developing world, with Latin American churches the most receptive. As noted in Chapter V, by the year 2000, over 11 percent of Catholics worldwide identified themselves as Charismatics, with a reported 8,771,000 Catholic Charismatics in Africa (7%), 16,422,000 in Asia (15%), 73,604,000 in Latin America (16%), some 350,000 in Oceania (4%), and even 100 in Antarctica (7%).[4]

Unlike the Pentecostal movement, which began among blue-collar Americans in California during the early 20th century, the CCR emerged among white, middle class college students during the tumultuous 1960s. But like the Pentecostal movement, the CCR has demonstrated remarkable appeal among developing and disenfranchised groups. The CCR appears to offer a sense of empowerment and to fill a need for relative freedom of expression not found in traditional Catholicism, especially in the developing world. This perceived empowerment is particularly evident among women, who have been active in the movement as members and as leaders since its earliest days.

The growing popularity of Charismatic Christianity in the developing world and particularly in Latin America has implications for Christianity in the United States. In 2007, the Pew Forum on Religion and Public Life reported that "Hispanics are transforming the nation's religious landscape, especially the Catholic Church, not only because of their growing numbers but also because they are practicing a distinctive form of Christianity." The "distinctive form" of Christianity to which the authors of the study refer is, of course, Charismatic Christianity. The authors reported that "more than half of Hispanic Catholics identify themselves as charismatics, compared with only an eighth of non-Hispanic Catholics."[5] Where the early participants in the CCR were mostly white, middle class college students, the Charismatic spirit in the United States seems to have shifted toward the growing number of Latino Catholic immigrants.

WORLDWIDE POPULARITY OF THE CCR

The dramatic expansion and increase in popularity enjoyed by the CCR in the developing world during the 1990s and in the first decade of the 21st century seems due, at least in part, to the ability of the movement to adapt to different cultures and to provide a "contextualized Christianity"[6] in areas whose cultures are distinctly different from the historically Western European branch of Catholicism. In addition to the marginalized societies in developing nations, the CCR has also offered women everywhere a degree of empowerment not normally seen in the Catholic church. From its earliest moments, the CCR has been driven by women working alongside their male co-Renewalists to spread the message of the Spirit. At a time when the church has been criticized for its refusal to permit women to serve as priests or to hold positions of authority, the democratizing influence of the CCR offers women, and the laity in general, validation and a way to feel useful and powerful within the Catholic church community.[7]

In a global society, it is difficult to overestimate the importance of religion and religious sentiment. Any historical study of the 20th century would be incomplete without a considerable amount of attention given to the religious trends and developments of the period. Protestant Pentecostalism and the CCR represented important new religious developments, first in American society, then later in world societies.

NOTES

1. *Ecumenism* denotes a movement that promotes unity among the various Christian denominations.
2. Mansfield, *As By a New Pentecost,* 16-19.
3. Ibid., 14.
4. World Christian Encyclopedia (accessed 31 May 2008); available from: http://www.iccrs.org/CCR%20worldwide.htm; Internet.
5. The Pew Forum on Religion and Public Life. Changing Faiths: Latinos and the Transformation of American Religion; (accessed 14 September 08); available from: http://pewforum.org/surveys/hispanic/; Internet.
6. Anderson, *An Introduction to Pentecostalism,* 122.
7. Philip Sheldrake, in *A Brief History of Spirituality* (Malden: Blackwell, 2007) pp. 202-204, refers to the idea of "making spirituality democratic" in the Catholic Charismatic Movement; however, he examines it from the perspective of a communal spirituality of all Catholics. He does not address the empowerment of women and other marginalized groups.

Selected Bibliography

INTERNET

http://www.cursillo.org/. Web site of the National Cursillo Center.
http://pewforum.org/surveys/pentecostal/?gclid=COLb6bK2u4kCFUE-GgodYj7UNA. Pew forum survey on Pentecostals and Charismatics.
http://www.ccr.org.uk/duquesne.htm. "GOODNEWS ONLINE": Web site of the CCR in England, Wales, Scotland, and Ireland.
www.worldchristiandatabase.org. World Christian Database. Web site maintained by the Center for the Study of Global Christianity.
http://www.welshrevival.org/newspapers/1955.03wm.htm. Web site of the Welsh Revival Library.
http://www.pastornet.net.au/renewal/fire/ff-1900.htm. Internet source of book, "Flashpoints of Revival." (Revival Press)
http://cursillos.ca/en/faq/f05-ultreya.htm. Web site of the Francophone Cursillo Movement of Canada.
http://www.landscaper.net/draft/0-72.htm#Induction%20Statistics. Web site of the 15th Field Artillery Regiment.
http://www.ewtn.com/library/COUNCILS/V1.HTM#1. Web site of the Eternal Word Television Network.
http://www.seattleu.edu/lemlib/web_archives/vaticanII/vaticanII.htm. The Second Vatican Council Resource Guide.
http://www.religion-cults.com/spirit/charismatic.htm#Popes_Statements. Independent web site of J. Dominguez, M.D.
http://www.iccrs.org/johnpaul_ii.htm. International Catholic Charismatic Renewal Renewal Services.
http://www.fraternityofsaintcharles.org/publications.cfm?id=95. Priestly Fraternity of the Missionaries of St. Charles Borromeo.
http://www.pastornet.net.au/renewal/fire/ff-1900.htm. *Flashpoints of Revival.* Web site devoted to making available primary source documents regarding religious revival.

Suenens, Leon Joseph. Malines Documents. Available from http://www.jcu.edu/suenens/pub.htm. Internet.

ARTICLES

Chestnut, R. Andrew. "A Preferential Option for the Spirit: The Catholic Charismatic Renewal in Latin America's New Religious Economy." *Latin American Politics and Society*, Vol. 45, No. 1, Spring, 2003, 55-85.

Francis, L. J. and M. Robbins. "Personality and Glossolalia: A Study Among Male Evangelical Clergy," *Pastoral Psychology*, Volume 51, Number 5, May 2003.

Gelpi, Don. "Discerning the Spirit among Catholic Charismatics" *dialog; a Journal of Theology.* Vol. 41, Number 1, Spring 2002.

Hughson, Thomas, S. J. "Interpreting Vatican II: A New Pentecost." *Theological Studies* 69 (March 2008). Available at http://goliath.ecnext.com/coms2/gi_0199-7640164/Interpreting-Vatican-II-a-new.html (8/8/08).

Johnson, C. Lincoln, Andrew J. Weigert. "An Emerging Faithstyle: A Research Note on the Catholic Charismatic Renewal. *Sociological Analysis*, Vol. 39, No. 2 Summer, 1978. 165-172.

O'Malley, John. "Reform, Historical Consciousness, and Vatican II's Aggiornamento," *Theological Studies* 32 (1971).

The Western Mail, 10 March 1955. "The Day that Evan Roberts Started the Flame." Available at: http://www.welshrevival.org/newspapers/1955.03wm.htm. Newspaper article about the Welsh religious revival of the 1950's.

BOOKS

General American Religious

Albanese, Catherine. *America: Religions and Religion.* Belmont: Wadsworth, 1992. One of the most comprehensive and widely used college textbooks on the history of religion and religious thought and movements in the United States.

Anderson, Allan. *An Introduction to Pentecostalism.* Cambridge: Cambridge University Press, 2004. An introduction to the Pentecostal tradition.

Bord, Richard J. and Joseph E. Faulkner. *The Catholic Charismatics: The Anatomy of a Modern Religious Movement.* Pennsylvania State University, 1983. Influential study of the early history of the Catholic Charismatic Renewal.

Bulman, Raymond F. *The Lure of the Millennium: The Year 2000 and Beyond.* Maryknoll: Orbis Books, 1999. Survey of millennial movements throughout human history, with a focus on millennialism in the modern world.

Stanley M. Burgess, ed. *The New International Dictionary of Pentecostal and Charismatic Movements.* Grand Rapids: Zondervan, 2002. Encyclopedic collection of entries on the Pentecostal and Charismatic movements.

Cox, Harvey. *Fire From Heaven: The Rise of Pentecostal Spirituality and the Reshaping of Religion in the Twenty-first Century.* Cambridge: Da Capo Press, 1995. Influential study of the origins of Pentecostal spirituality and its relationship to the modern world.

The Cursillo Weekend. An Official Publication of the National Secretariat. Dallas: The National Cursillo Center. Brief handbook of the Cursillo movment describing the process of the weekend Cursillo program.

Edwin S. Gaustad and Mark A. Noll, eds. *A Documentary History of Religion in America since 1877.* Grand Rapids: Wm. B. Eerdmans Publishing Co., 2003 Collection of primary source materials relating to the historical development of religion in the United States. Also includes some historical analysis.

Ellwood, Robert. *The Sixties' Spiritual Awakening.* (New Brunswick, NJ: Rutgers University Press, 1994). Study of the spirituality of the 1960's generation.

Goen, C. C. *Broken Churches, Broken Nation: Denominational Schisms and the Coming of the Civil War.* (Macon, GA: Mercer University Press, 1985). Historical study of the divisions in American Christianity in the period leading up to the Civil War.

Harper, Michael. *Three Sisters: A provocative look at Evangelicals, Charismatics, and Catholic Charismatics and their relationship to one another.* Wheaton: Tyndale House, 1979. Personal account of a pastor's experience with Pentecostal and Charismatic movements.

Heffner, Richard D. *A Documentary History of the United States.* New York: NewAmerican Library, 2002. Collection of primary source materials relating to United States history.

Holt, Bradley P. *Thirsty for God: A Brief History of Christian Spirituality.* Minneapolis: Fortress Press, 2005. Historical survey of Christian spirituality.

Jamison, Leland A., and James Ward Smith. *Religion in American Life.* Princeton: Princeton University Press, 1961. Classic historical study of American religious ideas and their relationship to various aspects of American life including social, political, and religious perspectives.

Jenkins, Philip. *The Next Christendom: The Coming of Global Christianity.* Oxford: Oxford University Press, 2002. Study of the history of global Christianity and its possible effects on the modern world.

———. *The New Faces of Christianity: Believing the Bible in the Global South.* Oxford: Oxford University Press, 2006. Examination of the development of Christianity in the developing world.

Kildahl, John P. *The Psychology of Speaking in Tongues.* New York: Harper & Row, 1972. Very influential examination of the psychology of glossolalia.

Marty, Martin E. *Modern American Religion, Vols. 1, 2, and 3.* Chicago: University of Chicago Press, 1986. One of the most respected and comprehensive studies of American religion and particularly American evangelicalism.

Maslow, A. H. *Religions, Values, and Peak-Experiences.* New York: Penguin, 1970. Classic psychological examination of religious experiences and their effects on the human psyche.

McWilliams, Wayne C. and Harry Piotrowski. *The World Since 1945: A History of International Relations.* Boulder: Lynne Rienner Publishers, 2005. Historical survey of the major themes in world history since the Second World War.

Raboteau, Albert. *Slave Religion: The Invisible Institution in the Ante-bellum South.*(New York: Oxford University Press, 1980). Study of the religious traditions and experiences of the African slaves in the United States.

Shattuck, Gardiner. *A Shield and a Hiding Place: The Religious Life of the Civil War Armies.* (Macon, GA: Mercer University Press, 1987). Examination of the religious life and practices of the Civil War armies.

Silk, Mark. *Spiritual Politics: Religion and America Since World War II.* (New York: Simon and Schuster, 1988). Study of religious life and practices in post-World War II America.

Smart, Ninian. *The Religious Experience.* New York: Macmillan, 1991. Examines the nature of religion and the problems regarding communication of religious experience. Included are examinations of Marxism and Humanism.

Whalen, Jack. *Beyond the Barricades: The Sixties Generation Grows Up.* Philadelphia: Temple University Press, 1989. Presentation of the ways in which the ideals and dreams of the generation of the 1960s evolved into the 1980s. Good source of historical and ideological background concerning the 1960s.

Wolfe, Alan. *The Transformation of American Religion: How We Actually Live Our Faith.* New York: Free Press, 2003. Examines the impact of religious thought on American society as it relates to American individualism and secularism.

Williams, Peter. *America's Religions: Traditions and Cultures.* (New York: Macmillan, 1990). Study of religious culture and traditions in America.

The Roman Catholic Charismatic Context

Bagiackas, Joseph. *The Future Glory: The Charismatic Renewal and the Implementation of Vatican II.* South Bend: Charismatic Renewal Services, Inc., 1983.
Study of the relationship between the CCR and the Second Vatican Council.

Bettenson, Henry and Chris Maunder, eds. *Documents of the Christian Church, New Edition.* New York: Oxford, 1999. Collection of primary source materials in church history.

Bord, Richard J. and Joseph E. Faulkner. *The Catholic Charismatics: The Anatomy of a Modern Religious Movement.* Pennsylvania State University Press, 1983. Historical analysis of the Catholic Charismatic Renewal.

Raymond F. Bulman, and Frederick J. Parrella, eds. *From Trent to Vatican II: Historical and Theological Investigations.* New York: Oxford, 2006. Deals with the continuity and the changes between the councils of Trent and Vatican II. Offers insights regarding challenges faced by modern Christianity.

Coppa, Frank, ed. *The Modern Papacy Since 1789.* Reading: Addison Wesley Publishing Company, 1998. Study of the papacy in modern times.

———. *Encyclopedia of the Vatican and Papacy.* Westport: Greenwood Press, 1999. Comprehensive encyclopedia on the papacy and the Vatican.

———. *The Papacy Confronts the Modern World.* Malabar: Krieger Publishing Company, 2003. Examines the responses of the papacy to liberalism, socialism and communism as well as historical events from the French Revolution to the Cold War.

Cordes, Paul Josef. *Call to Holiness: Reflections on the Catholic Charismatic Renewal.* Collegeville: The Liturgical Press, 1997. Reflections on the CCR written by an archbishop who was Vice-President of the Pontifical Council for the Laity from 1981-1996. He also served for ten years as the Episcopal Advisor to the International Catholic Charismatic Renewal Office in Rome, and later as President of the Pontifical Council *Cor Unum.*

Ford, J. Massyngberde. *Which Way for Catholic Pentecostals?* New York: Harper and Row, 1976. A noted charismatic describes the two types of Pentecostalism between which Catholics increasingly must choose.

Hummel, Charles E. *Fire in the Fireplace: Charismatic Renewal in the Nineties.* Downers Grove: InterVarsity Press, 1993. Historical analysis of the Catholic Charismatic Renewal, with a special emphasis on changes occurring in the 1990s.

Mansfield, Patti Gallagher. *As By a New Pentecost: The Dramatic Beginning of the Catholic Charismatic Renewal.* Singapore: Noah's Ark Creations Pte Ltd: 2002. Account of one of the original participants in the "Duquesne Weekend" which marks the beginning of the Catholic Charismatic Renewal.

Martin, Ralph. *The Fulfillment of All Desire: A Guidebook for the Journey to God Based on the Wisdom of the Saints.* (Steubenville: Emmaus Road Publishing, 2006. Written by one of the original members of the CCR, who was also a member of the Cursillo movement.

McDonnell, K. *Open the Windows. The Popes and the Charismatic Renewal.* South Bend, Indiana, 1989. Treatment of the relationship between the early CCR and the papacy.

Morris, Charles R. *American Catholic: The Saints and Sinners Who Built America's Most Powerful Church.* (New York: Random House, 1997). Study of the Catholics who were most influential in the American church.

National Conference of Catholic Bishops. "A Pastoral Statement of the Catholic Charismatic Renewal." March 1984. One of the early official episcopal responses to the CCR in the United States.

O'Connor, Edward D., C..S.C. *The Pentecostal Movement in the Catholic Church.* Notre Dame, Indiana: Ave Maria Press, 1971. Early study of the emerging CCR.

Ranaghan, Kevin and Dorothy. *Catholic Pentecostals.* New York: Paulist Press, 1969. Early study of the emerging CCR written by two members of the movement.

Vennari, John. *Close-ups of the Charismatic Movement.* Los Angeles: Tradition in Action, Inc., 2002. Analytical evaluation of the Catholic Charismatic Renewal.

Wead, R. Douglas. *Catholic Charismatics: Are they for real?* Carol Stream: Creation House, 1973. Personal account of a Protestant's experience with the Catholic Charismatic Renewal.

The Protestant/Evangelical Context

Anderson, Allan. *An Introduction to Pentecostalism.* Cambridge: Cambridge University Press, 2004. Examines the expansion of Pentecostalism with a special emphasis on the non-western expressions of the movement.

Balmer, Randall. *Blessed Assurance: A History of Evangelicalism in America.* Boston: Beacon Press, 1999. An excellent survey of Evangelical Christianity in the United States.

Beale, David O. *In Pursuit of Purity: American Fundamentalism Since 1850.* Greenville: Unusual Publications, 1986. Historical analysis of the origins of American Fundamentalism since 1850.

Boyer, Paul S. *When Time Shall Be No More: Prophecy Belief in Modern American Culture.* Cambridge: Belknap/Harvard University Press, 1992. A classic examination of the ways in which belief in biblical prophecy have affected American culture.

Stanley M. Burgess, ed. And Eduard M. Van Der Maas, Associate Editor. *The New International Dictionary of Pentecostal Charismatic Movements.* Grand Rapids: Zondervan, 2002.

Christian History Magazine 58 (Vol. XVII, No. 2). Evangelical Christian publication concerning the history of Christianity in its various forms.

Cox, Harvey. *Fire From Heaven: The Rise of Pentecostal Spirituality and the Reshaping of Religion in the Twenty-First Century.* Cambridge: Da Capo Press, 2001. An excellent examination of the rise and spread of global Pentecostalism.

Goff, James R., James R. Goff, Jr., Grant Wacker. *Portraits of a Generation: Early Pentecostal Leaders.* University of Arkansas Press, 2002.

Hayford, Jack W. and S. David Moore. *The Charismatic Century: The Enduring Impact of the Azusa Street Revival.* New York: TimeWarner, 2006. Historical review of the Pentecostal and Charismatic movements of the Twentieth Century.

Larry E. Martin, ed. *Holy Ghost Revival on Azusa Street: The True Believers. Eye Witness Accounts of the Revival that Shook the World.* Pensacola: Christian Life Books, 1998. Collection of eyewitness testimonies to the Azusa Street Revival in Los Angeles.

Los Angeles Times, 18 April 1906, "Weird Babel of Tongues," pg. I11. New York Times article regarding the Azusa Street Mission.

Marsden, George. *Fundamentalism and American Culture: The Shaping of Twentieth-Century Evangelicalism 1870-1925.* Oxford: Oxford University Press, 1980. Comprehensive sociological examination of the development of evangelicalism in the United States during the late nineteenth and early twentieth centuries.

Sherrill, John. *They Speak with Other Tongues.* Chosen: 2004. Influential study of the history of speaking in tongues.

Synan, Vinson. *The Century of the Holy Spirit: 100 Years of Pentecostal and Charismatic Renewal.* Nashville: Thomas Nelson Publishers, 2001. Comprehensive historical account of 20th-Century Pentecostal and Charismatic movements.

———. *Holiness-Pentecostal Tradition: Charismatic Movements in the Twentieth Century.* Grand Rapids: 1997. Analytical survey of 20th-Century Charismatic Movements.

The Pew Forum on Religion and Public Life. *Spirit and Power: A 10-Country Survey of Pentecostals*. Published October 2006. Comprehensive survey of Pentecostal and Charismatic movements and membership worldwide.

Wilkerson, David, with John and Elizabeth Sherrill, *The Cross and the Switchblade*. Jove, 1986. Novel that was a major influence on the emergence of the CCR.

Papal Documents and Addresses

Pope John Paul II. *Christifideles laici*. Post-synodal (1987 Synod of Bishops) apostolic exhortation. 1988.

Pope Paul VI. *Evangelii nuntiandi*. Apostolic exhortation. 1975.

Pope Pius IX *Syllabus of Errors* (in *Cuanta Cura*). Encyclical. 1864.

Pope Pius XII *Humani Generis*. Encyclical. 1950.

Pope John XXIII. *Prayer to the Holy Spirit* (1961). Opening prayer, Second Vatican Council (accessed 6 June 2008). Available from: http://www.dovcharismaticrenewal.org/cr_views.html; Internet.

Pope John Paul II. *Dominum et Vivificantem*. Encyclical. 1986.

Pope Paul VI. *Lumen Gentium*. Dogmatic Constitution on the Church. 1964.

Address of Pope John Paul II to the participants in the national Congress of the Italian "Renewal in the Spirit." Rimini, 14 March 2002. (accessed 6 June 2008). Available from: http://www.iccrs.org/johnpaul_ii.htm; Internet.

Address of Pope Benedict XVI to Communion and Liberation Pilgrimage Participants, St. Peter's Square, 14 March 2007. (accessed 6 June 2008). Available from: http://www.fraternityofsaintcharles.org/publications.cfm?id=95; Internet.

Address of His Holiness Pope Benedict XVI to Communion and Liberation Pilgrimage Participants. St. Peter's Square, 14 March 2007. (accessed 6 June 2008). Available from: http://www.fraternityofsaintcharles.org/publications.cfm?id=95; Internet.

Index

Acts: 2:1-4, 8, 63; 2:3-4, 65; 2:17-18, 8; 4:20, 58
Africa: contextualized Christianity in, 17–18; Pentecostal movement in, 16
Aggiornamento, 3, 36–37
ahimsa (non-violent resistance), 6
American Pentecostal movement, 4
American Protestants, 7
Anderson, Allan, 15, 17–18
Angelus Temple, 12
Antioch Weekend, 26
anti-war demonstrations, 5, 73
Apostolican Actuositam, 38
Apostolic Faith Mission, 16
Ark and Dove Retreat House, 52
As By a New Pentecost (Gallaher), 27
Asia, Pentecostal movement in, 16
Assembléa de Deus (Assembly of God), 16
Augustine of Hippo, 69
Australia, Pentecostal movement in, 16
auxiliary, 26
Azusa Street Mission, women in, 12
Azusa Street Revival, 2, 10–11, 70

baptism in the Spirit, 2, 10, 65
The Beatles, 6
Benedict XVI (pope), 2–3; on CCR, 42–43

Berg, Daniel, 16
Bethel Bible College, mission statement of, 12
von Bingen, Hildegard, 70
birth control, Suenens on, 39
Bonnín Aguiló, Eduardo, 23
Bord, Richard, on CCR objective, 38
Brazil, Pentecostal movement in, 15–16
breath, spirit and, 63
Bredesen, Harald: experiences of, 32; invitation of, 33; Mansfield and, 55–56
Buddhism, 6
Bullard, Ray, 55

Canadian Cursillos, 23–24
Catholic Action Diocesan Council, 23
Catholic Apostolic Church, 66
Catholic Charismatic Conference, 64–65
Catholic Charismatic Renewal (CCR), 2, 19, 38, 70–71; Benedict XVI on, 42–43; condemnation of, 44; demographic changes in, 58–61; early years of, 56, 73; evolution of, 55; Garcia on, 44, 59; growth of, 58, 74–76; history of, 4, 74; John Paul II and, 42; key documents/ideas impacting, 37; in Latin America, 59–60; *Magna Carta* of,

38; National Service Committee of, 57; papal responses to, 41–45; Pentecostalism v, 75; place within church of, 42; Pope Paul VI on, 41–42; Roman Catholic Church and, 3; Suenens on, 40–41; Vatican and, 40; women in, 76
Catholic Charismatics, 21n39, 64; early, 55, 74; experience of, 44–45; identification as, 59, 75; in Latin America, 59–60, 75; self-perception of, 33
The Catholic Charismatics: The Anatomy of a Modern Religious Movement (Bord and Faulker), 38
Catholic Charismatic spiritualities, 64–65, 68–71
Catholics, Protestants v., 43–44
Catholic spirituality, 70
Catholic tradition, 69
CCR. *See* Catholic Charismatic Renewal
centralization, ecumenism and, 55–57
Charismatic Christianity, popularity of, 75–76
charismatic gifts, importance of, 40
Charismatic prayer groups, marginalization of, 44
Charismatic spirituality, 70; nature of, 4. *See also* Catholic Charismatic spiritualities
charisms, 4, 40, 43, 61, 64; ambivalence about, 69; intentions for, 44; during medieval period, 70. *See also* gift of healing; gift of tongues; prophecy
Chestnut, Andrew R., 59; on Pentecostalism, 60
Chile, Pentecostal movement in, 15
China, WWII casualties of, 4
Chi Rho Society, 6–7, 34n20, *50*; Mansfield in, 27
Christianity, contextualized, 17–18, 76
Christifideles Laici, 38, 59

Church of God in Christ (COGIC), 11
civil rights movement, 1, 5–6, 73
Clark, Steve, 1–3; experiences of, 32; influence of, 75; Martin and, 57; on psychological pressure, 26
clerical celibacy, 40
COGIC. *See* Church of God in Christ
cold-war conflicts, 1, 5
Collins, Peter, 70
Congregação Cristã, 16
Congregacioni Christiani, 16
contextualized Christianity, 76; in Africa, 17–18
continued identity, 27
Cordes, Paul Josef, 26–27, 58, 60, 68
Cox, Harvey: on healing, 60; on independent Christian churches, 18; on receptivity, 17
The Cross and the Switchblade (Wilkerson), 28
Cuban Missile Crisis (1962), 5
cursillista, 24, 25
cursillo (short course), 2, 23; popularity of, 3, 24; program, 24–27, 75; psychological pressure in, 26; stages of, 24; themes of, 25
Cursillo movement, 1–2, 19, 23–27, 32

Diocesan Renewal Centers, 57
Dionysius, 69
Dodge, Flo, 3, 21n39, 32, 55, 74
Dogmatic Constitution On The Catholic Faith, 36
Dominum et Vivificantem, 38
draft. *See* Selective Service System
Duquesne University, *49*
Duquesne Weekend, 1–2, 7, 19, 27–30, 32, *48*, *51*, 55

Eastern Orthodox Christianity, 64
Eastern religions, 73
Easwaran, Eknath, 6
ecumenical council, 36, 45n1
ecumenical ideal, 56

ecumenical unity, 60–61
ecumenism, 74; centralization and, 55–57
Emmaus Walk, 23
empowerment, 75; gift of healing and, 60; Pentecostalism and, 17–19
establishment values, 6
Evangelii Nuntiandi, 58
evangelization: in 1980s/1990s, 57; early, 32–33; papal support for, 59; role of, 58

Faulker, Joseph, on CCR objective, 38
Fellowship of Communities of Evangelization in the Holy Spirit, 58
feminist movement, 1, 5, 73
FGBMFI. *See* Full Gospel Business Men's Fellowship International
Finney, Charles, 9
1 Corinthians: 12:7, 39; 12:11, 39; 13, 64; 15, 64
First Dogmatic Constitution on the Church of Christ, 36
First Vatican Council (1869-1870), 36
Ford, J. Massyngberde, 44, 47n22
Francescon, Luigi, 16
Full Gospel Business Men's Fellowship International (FGBMFI), 55

Galatians 3-5, 64
Gallagher, Patti. *See* Mansfield, Patti Gallagher
Gandhi, Mahatma, 6
Garcia, Miguel, on CCR, 44, 59
Germany, WWII casualties of, 4
gift of healing, 13, 67; Cox on, 60; empowerment and, 60; Mansfield and, 31, 68. *See also* charisms
gift of tongues: evidence of, 15; in Mangan, 31, 66; in Mansfield, 31. *See also* charisms; *glossolalia*; *xenolalia*
Glory of God Covenant Community, 58
glossolalia (speaking in tongues), 4, 10, 60; ambivalence towards, 69; definition of, 19n11; documented cases of, 70; psychological study of, 65–66. *See also* charisms; gift of tongues; *xenolalia*
Gray, Paul, 65
Greece, WWII casualties of, 4

healing, gift of. *See* gift of healing
Hervas, Juan, 24
Hindu traditions, 6
Hispanic Catholics, 75
Holiness Methodists, 9; women and, 12
Holy Spirit: call to, 37–41; common experience of, 61; in ecumenical terms, 56; life in, 64; as origin, 43; personal relationship with, 4, 64–65; signs of, 68–69; Suenens on, 40
Hoover, Willis Collins (1858-1936), 15
Hughson, Thomas, 37
Humani Generis, 36

ICCRO. *See* International Catholic Charismatic Renewal Office
Iglesia Metodista Pentecostal (Methodist Pentecostal Church), 15
India, Pentecostal movement in, 16
Indonesia, Pentecostal movement in, 16–17
inspiration, 63
International Catholic Charismatic Renewal Office (ICCRO), 57
International Catholic Programme of Evangelization, 58
International Conference on the Catholic Charismatic Renewal, 41
Irving, Edward, 66

Jaramillo, Diego, 59
Jenkins, Philip, 60
John of the Cross, 70
John Paul II (pope), 2–3; CCR and, 42
John XXIII (pope), 3, 36, 45n5, 45n7

King, Martin Luther, Jr., 6

laity, responsibilities of, 40
latihan, 35n40
Latin America: Catholic Charismatics in, 59–60, 75; CCR in, 59–60; Pentecostal movement in, 15
Lopez, Antonio, 44, 59–60
Lumen Gentium, 38; Article 12, 39, 45n10

Mahan, Asa, 9
Maharishi Mahesh Yogi, 6
Malines documents, 56
Mangan, David, 29, *54*; gift of tongues and, 31, 66
Mansfield, Patti Gallagher, 2–3, 7, 21n39, *53*, *54*, 74; biography of, 27–28; Bredesen and, 55–56; desires of, 28–29, 73; on discovering the church, 38–39; experience of, 29, 35n40, 65; on first conference, 58; gift of healing and, 31, 68; gift of tongues and, 31; guidance prayer of, 33; influence of, 75; memoirs of, 26; messages recorded by, 30–31; on Vatican II documents, 39
Marshall Plan, 5
Martin, Ralph, 1–2; campus ministry of, 33; Clark and, 57; on continuing participation, 26; cursillo participation of, 3; experiences of, 32; influence of, 75; Pope Paul VI and, 40–41; qualifications of, 34n16
McPherson, Aimee Semple, 12; kidnapping of, 13
McPherson, Harold, 12
medicine man, 71n19
Methodist Church, 9–10, 12, 15
military draft. *See* Selective Service System
modernity, threat of, 36
Morgan, M. P., 14
Movimiento de Cursillos de Cristiandad, 23

Mutmansky, Marybeth, 32, 65

Neocharismatics, 21n39, 21n44
New International Dictionary of Pentecostal and Charismatic Movements, 24
New Year Bible Study course (1907), 15
1960s, 1, 73; religious/social environment of, 4–7
nuclear arms race, 5

O'Malley, John, 36–37

Palmer, Phoebe, 9
Parham, Charles Fox, 10
Pauline spirituality, 63–64
Paul VI (pope), 2–3, 24, 58; on CCR, 41–42; on evangelization, 59; Martin and, 40–41
PAW. *See* Pentecostal Assemblies of the World
Penance Service, 28
Pentecostal Assemblies of the World (PAW), 11
Pentecostalism/Pentecostal movement, 2, 4, 73, 76; attraction to, 60; beginning of, 8–12; CCR v., 75; Chestnut on, 60; in the developing world, 17; empowerment and, 17–19; global expansion of, 14–17; *glossolalia* in, 66; roots of, 9; women in, 12–14, 18
Pentecostals, 64; Catholics v., 43–44; definition of, 21n39
pilgrimage, 2–3
Pius IX (pope), 36
Pius XII (pope), 36
pneuma (breath/spirit), 63
Poland, WWII casualties of, 4
poor, theology of, 17–18, 60
postcursillo, 24, 26
prana (breath/spirit), 63
Prayer to the Holy Spirit (John XXIII), 45n5, 45n7

precursillo, 24–25
prophecy, 67
Protestant churches, 70
Protestant Pentecostals. *See* Pentecostals

Raassina, Hanna, 16
Raassina, Verner, 16
racism, 11
Ramabai, Pandita, 14–15
Ransil, Elaine Kersting, 26
The Ranters, 66
Ratuwalu, Johannes, 17
resurrection of Jesus, 64
Roberts, Evan, 14
rollos (talks), 24
Roman Catholic Church, 64; CCR and, 3; renewal of, 1–2
Roman Catholic Cursillo movement, 3
Romans 3-8, 64
ruach (wind), 63

Saint Paul, first letter to Corinthians of, 69
sanctification, 9, 14
Santiago de Campostela, 2
satsangs (spiritual gatherings), 35n40
satyagraha philosophy, 6, 7n8
Scanlan, Michael, 57
Scanlon, Gina, 29
Second Vatican Council (1962-1965). *See* Vatican II
Selective Service System (military draft), 5
Semple, Robert, 12
Seymour, William J., 10–11
shaman, 71n19
Sherrill, John, 32, 70
Sixties Generation, 5
social Darwinism, 11
Soviet Union, WWII casualties of, 4–5
Spanish *Cursillo* movement, 2. *See also Cursillo* movement
speaking in tongues. *See* gift of tongues
Spirit. *See* Holy Spirit
spirit, breath and, 63

spirituality: apophatic/hesychastic, 64, 71n3; Catholic, 70; charismatic, 4, 64–65, 68–71; kataphatic, 64, 71n3; Pauline, 63–64
spiritual renewal, 73
spiritual search, 6
Springel, Maryann, 65
Stalin, Josef, Marshall Plan rejection by, 5
Stevens African Methodist Episcopal Church, 10
Subud, 35n40
Suenens, Leon Joseph, 2, 73; appointment of, 56; on CCR, 40–41; on Holy Spirit, 40; as progressive voice, 39–40
Sunday, Billy, 13
surrender, attitude of, 65
Syllabus of Errors, 36
Synod of Bishops, 61n22

Talavera, Carlos, 59
Talfan Davies, Aneirin, 14
Teresa of Avila, 70
theology of the poor, 17–18, 60
They Speak with Other Tongues (Sherrill), 32, 70
tongues, gift of. *See* gift of tongues
Truman Doctrine, 5

ultreya (onward), 24, 26
United Pentecostal Church, 11
United States, post-war economy of, 4

Vatican, CCR and, 40
Vatican II (1962-1965), 2, 33; documents of, 39; importance of, 37; mood preceding, 36–37; purpose of, 3, 37
Vietnam, 1, 5
Vingren, Gunnar, 16

Washtenaw Covenant Community, 57
Wesley, John (1703-1791), 2, 9
Whalen, Jack, 5–6

Wilkerson, David, 28, 32
witch doctor, 71n19
women: in Azusa Street Mission, 12; in CCR, 76; Holiness Methodists and, 12; in Pentecostal movement, 12–14, 18
Woodworth-Etter, Maria Beulah, 12; divine healing campaigns of, 13
Word of God (Ann Arbor, MI), 57

World Christian Database, 8–9
World War II (WWII), 4

xenolalia (speaking in foreign tongues), 9–10, 20n11. *See also* charisms; gift of tongues; *glossolalia*

Yokum, Bruce, 57
Yugoslavia, WWII casualties of, 4

www.ingramcontent.com/pod-product-compliance
Lightning Source LLC
Chambersburg PA
CBHW030909040526
R18240000002B/R182400PG44116CBX00004B/3